CHILD DEVELOPMENT

VOLUME TWO

Universal Stage

of Infancy

THE CENTURY PSYCHOLOGY SERIES

Richard M. Elliott, Gardner Lindzey, & Kenneth MacCorquodale

Editors

CHILD DEVELOPMENT

VOLUME TWO

Universal Stage of Infancy

BY

Sidney W. Bijou
UNIVERSITY OF ILLINOIS
AND
Donald M. Baer
UNIVERSITY OF KANSAS

New York

APPLETON-CENTURY-CROFTS
Division of Meredith Publishing Company

For information address the publisher, Appleton-Century-Crofts, Division of Meredith Publishing Company, 440 Park Avenue South, New York, N.Y. 10016

6115-6

Library of Congress Card Number: 61-14365

PRINTED IN THE UNITED STATES OF AMERICA

E 09264

PREFACE

In Volume I of *Child Development*, we presented a system of concepts and principles to describe the process of behavioral development. We defined development as progressive changes in interactions between a child's responses and the stimulus events and setting conditions which make up his environment.

In this volume we begin the application of these concepts and principles to the initial development of the human infant. In order to set boundaries to this task, we have chosen as our starting point that stage in gestation at which the fetus responds as a unified system to external stimuli; as our end-point that stage (usually in the second year) during which the symbolizing function begins to emerge. The first point was chosen because we wanted our account of development to begin with the inception of psychological behavior. The end-point was chosen because the symbolizing function has broad and profound consequences in the child's later behavior; the pre-symbolic child is so different from the symbolic child that separate treatment is practically mandatory.

This analysis has been difficult to make, particularly with respect to fetal and neonatal development. Questions far outnumbered factual answers, and the choice between ignoring a topic and critizing its current nebulous state was not easy. We trust we have exercised deliberate moderation. We have indicated that many areas urgently need experimental analysis. At the same time, we have tried to avoid obscuring the potential power of a natural science analysis by *not* dwelling on what is *not* known. With the same ambition, we have tried to point to examples of research which might contribute substantially to our understanding of child development.

Other problems have been more mechanical but no less vexing. Format was one of these. We wished to cover the usual topics of child development, even though the principles we have used do not readily lend themselves to such distinctions (for example, motor, intellectual, and social development). We also wished to emphasize the characteristics of the Universal stage (as Kantor describes it), not only to show its significance for organizing infant behavioral development, but also to provide a background for the treatment of the succeeding stages of development. We tried to scrutinize the literature of related fields for applicable documentation, experimental in nature and reliable in execution and outcome. In each instance compromise was frequent.

In all of this, we had wonderful assistance from our students and our colleagues. We are particularly indebted to Jay S. Birnbrauer, David D. Crowell, and Barbara C. Etzel for reviewing the chapters, to Shirley Shapiro and Anona Bangs for preparing the revisions of the manuscript, and to Kenneth MacCorquodale for suggesting ways of improving the presentation. We also wish to express our indebtedness to the National Institute of Mental Health, United States Public Health Service, for providing funds for research in normal and deviant development (MH-02208 and MH-02232). Much of our thinking has been generated and advanced by the research programs the National Institute of Mental Health has made possible.

S. W. B.
D. M. B.

CONTENTS

CHILD DEVELOPMENT

VOLUME TWO

Universal Stage of Infancy

1

The Universal Stage of Development

Volume I of *Child Development* presented a systematic and empirical theory of behavior development, and included examples from everyday situations to clarify the theoretical principles advanced. This volume begins the systematic application of these principles to the initial sequences of child development, from prenatal interactions through the second year of the child's life, roughly to the point at which symbolic behavior becomes prominent.

The acquisition of efficient symbolic behavior profoundly alters the character of a child's interaction with his environment. This alone would be sufficient reason for choosing the time prior to his symbolic functioning as a unit for analysis and discussion. There are, however, even more compelling reasons. Kantor (1959a, 1959b) showed that behavior development may be viewed as a sequence of three general periods of interaction between the organism, his biological characteristics, and the environment. Kantor called these intervals the Universal, Basic, and Societal stages.[1] This volume is concerned with the Universal stage, which is similar in several respects to the sensory-motor period of Piaget (1954), Flavell (1963), and Werner (1948).

In this account of the Universal stage, as in Volume I, we shall continue to consider development from a naturalistic point of view. To do so, we must observe the behavior of children and events which are related to that behavior. Both the behavior and the related events will always have physical dimensions

[1] In his earlier writings, Kantor referred to the Universal stage as the Foundational stage.

(or we would not be able to observe them); but their physical characteristics alone would not bring them to our attention for psychological analysis. It is always the *relationship* between them which provides a subject matter. A sleeping child may move an arm; if we can observe no event classifiable as a reason for the response, we have no way of categorizing it in a more understandable manner. If, however, a fly had settled on that arm, and the arm moved *in response,* we then would have a simple but meaningful interaction. Investigation might readily show us that the tactual stimulation produced by the fly set the occasion for the response and that the significant characteristic of the response was that it drove the fly away and stopped the tactual stimulation. On the other hand, had a fly settled on an arm of the sleeping child and no response were then observed, there would be no point in considering the fly as a stimulus event in the child's environment. Were the fly not there, the child's behavior would not be different. In short, a naturalistic account of psychological development considers behavior and other events only if they have both *physical* and *functional* characteristics; it does not consider behavior apart from related events, nor events apart from the behavior they effect.

The events to which behavior relates are called "environmental" and "organismic." Environmental events stimulate: they elicit, discriminate, and reinforce behavior, as, for example, words do for man. Organismic events establish a style and limitation to behavior, as feathers do for birds and fingers for man. Furthermore, organismic events prescribe the kinds and ranges of environmental events that may prove functional. Thus man looks at much of his environment but ingests relatively little of it; the earthworm does almost the reverse.

The essence of the Universal stage, Kantor pointed out, lies in the three distinctive ways in which developing behavior relates to organismic and environmental events. The first pattern pertains to the predominance of biological structure and physiological functioning in early behavioral interactions; the second, to the limited role of environmental stimuli in controlling simple but self-preserving respondents; and the third, to the emergence of behaviors related to, but not identical with maintaining the biological necessities of life. These patterns of development account for the organization of this volume. Let us look at them in more detail.

CHARACTERISTICS OF THE UNIVERSAL STAGE

Prevalence of Biological Behaviors

Initially, before birth the human organism is primarily a biological structure. It lives, assimilating raw materials into new and growing cells, maintaining more and more of its own processes, pumping its blood, moving its own limbs; and, after birth, doing its own breathing, regulating its heat level, disposing of waste products, and engaging in most of the other business of living. Much of this behavior is internal; the external environment is more typically *permissive,* rather than *prescriptive.* Given that the newborn is immersed in a suitable physical atmosphere, he will go on breathing it and using it internally as necessary. If food is placed in his mouth, he will ingest it, metabolize it, assimilate it, and dispose of the accompanying wastes.

These activities are complex and well organized, but their relationship to the external environment is simple: within a given range of external conditions, these activities go on; beyond that range, they falter or stop. At first, this seems to be all there is in the interaction between the new organism and his external environment. As the Universal stage proceeds, however, these interactions take a less dominant role in the child's total behavior. Obviously, they do not cease until death; but they are supplemented (and later swamped) by the increasing appearance of behavior which does interact in a close way with external environmental events. The development of these new interrelations is the second characteristic of the Universal stage.

Initial Development of Respondent and Operant Behaviors

During this stage, as the biological equipment of the infant matures, two classes of behavior emerge which either are closely tied to external stimulation or become so through experience. The first class consists of well-structured responses having a characteristic shape or topography. They are easily described and named (e.g., blinking, sucking, stretching, head-turning, the startle response, the patellar reflex, etc.) and readily recordable.

The second class of responses emerging during the Universal stage at first are vague, formless responses which rarely take even approximately the same form twice. They are difficult to name or describe. "Random," "uncoordinated," and "gross" are the terms generally applied in efforts to categorize them. These movements of the face, head, arms, and legs gradually take on form and precision as a consequence of increasing interactions with the environment. They evolve into skilled motor and verbal sequences or chains typical of the older child, adolescent, and adult.

The first class of behavior consisting of well-structured responses is activated by antecedent external stimulation and is usually insensitive to whatever stimulus consequences the behavior produces. Hence this behavior may be classified as respondent behavior. The second class, consisting initially of uncoordinated responses, is shaped by stimulus consequences and also becomes discriminated to antecedent stimuli which mark occasions for differential reinforcement contingencies. This second class of behavior may be described as operant behavior.

The initial respondent and operant interactions with the environment are closely related to the first characteristic of development during the Universal stage, i.e., biological interactions closely related to the processes of living and growing. Most of the respondents serve a protective function (or perhaps once did, in the evolutionary history of the organism), and thus contribute to the health and survival of the infant. Blinking protects the eye; the pupillary reflex preserves retinal cells from damage possible from strong light; yawning contributes to the oxygen supply. These respondent behaviors are strong not because of the mechanism of reinforcement but presumably because of the mechanism of evolutionary selection.

The operant responses of the infant acquire shape and chained complexity as the consequences of the stimuli they produce or remove. During the early part of the Universal stage the effective stimulus consequences consist of materials essential to the maintenance of life and health. Examples of reinforcing consequences which serve the biological functions of the infant and also strengthen the operant chains producing these events are food, water, taste properties of certain valuable body builders (such as sugar), the opportunity to breathe, and the opportunity to rest. Extremes of light, sound, and pressure are examples of reinforcing consequences which harm or disrupt the child's biological functioning and at the same time serve to strengthen the operant chains that remove such aversive stimuli from the child's environment. Stimuli which function in these two basic ways may be referred to as "primary" or "homeostatic" reinforcers.

Initial Elaboration of Ecological Behavior

The third characteristic of the Universal stage is development of ecological behavior. As the infant develops longer, more finely discriminated, and more minutely differentiated operant chains, a large class of stimuli begin to function as reinforcers. These "new" reinforcers have only an indirect relationship to the biological functioning and survival of the child. That is, these stimuli are not the things in his external environment which are required for life and health; they are the stimulus properties of other things, their characteristic shape, color, sound, and feel, which the child invariably interacts with in order to control the primary or homeostatic reinforcers himself. Food, for example, is a biological necessity. In the infant's world, food most often takes the form of milk. For a given infant, milk may come to him in a glass bottle with a rubber nipple. The stimulus properties of milk for this infant thus include what we know to be the stimulus properties of glass and rubber and of forms like the bottle. In the course of ingesting his milk, this infant learns about the feel of glass and rubber in hand and mouth, about the hand responses necessary to hold a nursing bottle, and the mouth responses which promote or retard the flow of liquid into his mouth. In short, because the biologically necessary stimuli have accompanying physical properties, behaviors controlled by those properties are more successful in securing the biological necessities. *Ultimately*, these behaviors are controlled by the final reinforcing contingency with a biological stimulus (such as the milk), but *initially*, they are controlled by the physical properties of milk bottles: glass cylinders of a given shape and weight.

Thus, observation shows the typical infant developing operant behavior more and more controlled (at the moment it occurs) simply by the physical properties of his environment. These are the discriminated and differentiated operants. For example, a child in his bath learns to cup his hands tightly together when playing with water, since that is the form of response which succeeds in holding and lifting water. He learns to strike the water with a flat palm because that response produces a sharp report and dramatic splash. He learns the scooping responses which displace the water in large quantities, and the capturing movement which takes a bubble of air below the surface. In short, with many of the things in his environment, he engages in behavior which succeeds more and more in manipulating and controlling his physical environment.

Kantor used the term "ecological" to label this characteristic of the interaction of behavior with properties of the environment. He said, "Psychological activities of the ecological type are concerned with the organism's becoming acquainted with its surrounding, learning what kinds of things exist and how to handle them" (Kantor, 1933). Thus, we may call the ecological properties of things "ecological reinforcers"; they appear to be secondary or acquired reinforcers, developed because they are the discriminative properties of biologically important (homeostatic) reinforcers.

Many of the "things" in an infant's environment are, of course, people. People obviously cannot be manipulated in the same way that water can. On the other hand, people usually are responsive to words, cries, gestures, and facial expressions such as smiles and frowns. Hence responses of this sort readily develop as another class of ecological behavior developed during the Universal stage.

It is clear that the development characteristic of the Universal stage is nearly universal in children. However, it is important to note that the standard nature of this learning derives partly from the inherent biological characteristics of the child as a representative of his species, and partly from certain characteristics of any environment necessary for his survival. It is not that these developments cannot be changed or altered; rather the biological and environmental processes which give rise to them are rarely within the power or the desire of man to change. In other words, children go through the Universal stage in such a uniform manner not so much because it is so decreed within their nature, but because given their nature, they learn certain skills invariably taught by both their physical and social environments.

PLAN OF PRESENTATION

We shall open our discussion with a brief consideration of development from conception to birth. By so doing we shall gain some idea of the history of the individual as a developing fetus. Such information allows continuity in the analysis of development after birth. For if we inquire into the nature of the interaction between biological and psychological processes *in utero,* we establish the context for the Universal stage to which we refer in the later discussions of postnatal development. More specifically, we can probe into the onset and significance of prenatal psychological activity and the effect of the birth process on subsequent environmental and behavioral changes. Prenatal development will therefore be the subject of Chapter 2.

In a consideration of postnatal development, it is essential in a naturalistic approach to survey stimulus-response interactions characteristic of the infant before he has had a long history with events of an external environment. Since birth makes these interactions available for detailed observation for the first time, Chapters 3 and 4 are concerned with a survey of the behavior of the newborn and the conditions and processes that operate to continue or change the behavior.

The basic mechanisms by which the behavior of the newborn becomes elaborated into the intricate interactions characteristic of the child, adolescent, and adult are discussed in Chapter 5. In that context, heredity, and respondent and operant processes are evaluated, and the ever-increasing importance of operant behavior is noted.

To understand how operant behavior is acquired and maintained, one must know which stimuli have reinforcing functions.

Thus, Chapter 6 is concerned with an analysis of the stimuli most likely to have or shortly to acquire reinforcing functions for newborn infants. We will present separately those stimuli which are quite likely to have reinforcing functions and those whose likelihood is more speculative. In particular, the development of a class of reinforcers involved in the control of the environment is considered, since this is the class of reinforcers which is at issue in the development and maintenance of ecological behavior. These reinforcers are referred to as "ecological reinforcers."

Given the prerequisites, an elaboration of motor development, including reaching, prehension, body management, and locomotion, appears in Chapter 7. Development of behavior to the social world (with emphasis on the relationship between the infant and the mother) appears in Chapter 8 and to the physical world in Chapter 9. In Chapter 10 an analysis is made of the development of verbal behavior. Since verbal behavior blossoms into symbolic functioning in its most prominent human form, it is placed near the end of the Universal stage. Finally in Chapter 11 an analysis is made of early emotional behavior.

It should be kept in mind that chapter categorizations of development are artificial and arbitrary. Separate discussions overlap each other; yet some topics require separate discussions when they do not readily integrate into an otherwise convenient progression of chapters. For these reasons, we point out here that Chapters 2, 3, and 4 offer precursors for psychological development. Chapters 5 and 6 discuss the underlying processes in development and elaboration and the stimulus operations integral to development in the Universal stage. Chapters 7, 8, 9, and 10 make up another division concerned primarily with the response aspect of development and the development of supporting reinforcers. The evolution of emotional behavior does not rest comfortably in either section; therefore, it is considered separately in Chapter 11.

Finally, the major points of this volume will be brought together in preparation for an analysis of the next period of development, the Basic stage, which includes the next three years of life and is therefore roughly equivalent to early childhood. An elaboration of a functional definition of this phase of development will be the subject of Volume III.

REFERENCES

Flavell, J. H. *The developmental psychology of Jean Piaget.* Princeton, N.J.: Van Nostrand, 1963.

Kantor, J. R. *Interbehavioral psychology.* (Rev. ed.) Bloomington, Ind.: Principia Press, 1959a. Pp. 165–169.

Kantor, J. R. Evolution and the science of psychology. *Psychol. Rec.,* 1959b, 9, 131–142.

Piaget, J. *The construction of reality in the child.* New York: Basic Books, 1954.

Werner, H. *Comparative psychology of mental development.* (Rev. ed.) Chicago: Follett, 1948.

2

Prenatal Development — Biological and Psychological

INTRODUCTION

In Volume I a convenient distinction was made between the subject matters of biology and psychology.

Biology, it was pointed out, is typically concerned with the anatomical structure and the physiological functioning of the parts of the body. That is, biology deals with the glands, muscles, bones, the connecting mechanisms of the body such as the nervous, circulatory, and endocrine systems, and with the interrelationships among these parts and systems.

Psychology, in contrast, is concerned with the *interactions of the complete, integral organism with environmental events.*

Kantor (1959) elaborated on this distinction:

> When we compare biology with psychology we find that in the former the evolutional changes and transformations are interconnected with an *entity or substantive form,* that is an organism, while in psychology the evolutional processes are *connected only with acts.* In biology current behavioral changes are functions of morphological or anatomical structure. In psychological activities the organism performing the activity is not structurally as important as the mutual interactions it performs in connection with other things (p. 134, italics ours).

Two points should be made about the relationships between biological and psychological phenomena: both classes of events take place at the same time, and each has effects on the other.

The organism is always interacting with an environment; and while some acts are more convenient to study than others, any act can be isolated for either psychological or biological analysis. For example, in a study of electric shock stimulation, an experimental psychologist might be interested in analyzing the conditions promoting consistent and reliable avoidance behavior to the stimulation; while a biologist might be interested in the interrelationships between heart and respiratory rates produced by noxious conditions of this sort. Usually, it is the organismic part of an act which is studied from the biological point of view.

Biological and psychological interactions indeed have effects on each other. Many biological events may constitute variables which influence psychological changes. However, biological events should not be considered the sole cause of psychological action. Instead they should be thought of as combining with physical and societal events to determine psychological action. Furthermore, the mechanisms of biological development are not identical to those of psychological development.[1]

The nature of the interdependencies between biological and psychological interactions may be illustrated in at least four ways:

1. Anatomical and physiological characteristics of the organism set limits on the classes of responses possible. Physical constraints of this sort serve to characterize species. The human organism cannot fly like a bird; a worm cannot play the piano.
2. Biological variables set limits on the range of responses at developmental stages, especially during immaturity (infancy and early childhood) and old age. Thus, an infant cannot stand erect and walk until his bones, tendons, and neuromuscular system are sufficiently developed to combat gravity effectively; a young child cannot make certain speech sounds until his teeth are present and functional; a person past 45 may have to learn to extend the distance between his eyes and the newspaper to read since his eyes no longer focus as they once did.
3. Biological activities of the organism produce internal stimuli comparable to external stimuli in that they too acquire stimulus functions. Gastric pains may be aversive, and behavior which eliminates them is strengthened. Neutral stimuli paired with such pains may, of course, acquire discriminative and reinforcing properties.
4. The anatomical and physiological characteristics of an individual

[1] Gesell, for example, has stated that they are: "The action systems of embryo, fetus, infant, and child undergo pattern changes which are so sequential and orderly that we may be certain that the patterning process is governed by mechanisms of form regulation—the same mechanisms which are being established by the science of embryology" (1954, p. 337).

provide stimuli to other people and thereby influence the kinds and amounts of social interactions he experiences. The pubescent boy undergoing a voice change might be subjected to mild aversive stimulation from his peers and temporarily avoid contacts with them. The unusually tall girl might develop a slumped posture in an effort to avoid teasing by her peers ("How's the climate up there?").

The interactions also go the other way: *psychological events influence biological events.* Social play may stimulate the young child to engage in vigorous running and skipping and thereby increase the growth rate of the large muscles. Likewise, psychological factors in the history of the individual and in the cultural practices of his parents may determine the amount and kind of food consumed which directly influence the growth of bone structure.

Thus, we see that the conditions which influence psychological functioning *include* variables which ordinarily are called biological, and the conditions which influence biological functioning *include* "psychological" variables. This statement of relationship between biological and psychological phenomena may be considered a special case of one of the most universal conclusions of scientists: *natural phenomena are never sensitive to a single, unitary condition or cause; multiple interactions of conditions are so typical as to be considered inevitable.* We make this point with such emphasis because of its particular relevance to developmental psychology, especially in the study of prenatal and infant development. Biological and psychological interrelationships appear to be more intimately related in these stages than in the others.

In discussing prenatal development, we shall address ourselves to the following four questions:

1. Do the variables which determine prenatal biological growth, giving the fetus its distinctive human form and function, relate to psychological development at the same time?
2. When may the human fetus meaningfully be called a psychological organism?
3. What are the psychological activities which occur during the prenatal period?
4. What is the relationship between birth and psychological development?

THE COURSE OF PRENATAL DEVELOPMENT

The anatomical structure of the fetus can be recognized as human in form by the second month; the initial formation of almost every essential biological aspect of the new individual takes place by the third month.

Some landmarks in the structural development of the fetus are outlined in the following tabulation from Arey (1954). The figures in parentheses refer to lunar months.

It is also possible to provide some landmarks in the progression of biological and psychological behaviors. In noting these transitions, it should be borne in mind that they are dependent to a great extent on the anatomical changes listed in Chart 2-1.

Perhaps one other reminder is essential: these data are from "prematures"—fetuses removed from the womb before full term. Whether or not findings on prematures may be said to pertain to the biological and psychological behavior of fetuses *in utero* is still a question.

Approximate behavior "onsets" from the 4th to the 20th week of fetal development (Hooker, 1952; Carmichael, 1951) usually include the following:

1. At about 4 weeks the heart starts beating at a regular rate.
2. At about 8 weeks the trunk and head movements are elicited by tactile stimulation.
3. At about 12 weeks brief "spontaneous" jerky movements are observed.
4. At about 20 weeks the sucking reflex and respiratory movements occur.

From about 28 weeks to the time of birth the number and kinds of activities increase at an accelerated rate. A comprehensive list drawn up by Gesell (1945) is shown in Chart 2-2.

What determines the anatomical and physiological sequences observed in a species? What accounts for the specific anatomical and physiological characteristics of a given individual? Unfortunately, no profound and detailed answer has been offered. A rough program of research can be suggested, however. In the early stages, consider physical and chemical factors of the uterine environment; in the later stages, consider physical, chemical, *and*

CHART 2-1

Anatomical Development IN UTERO in Terms of Lunar Months Given in Parentheses (Arey, 1954)

Integument	three-layered epidermis (3) body hair begins (4) skin glands form, sweat and sebaceous (4)
Mouth	lip fusion complete (2) palate fused completely (3) enamel and dentin depositing (5) primordia of permanent teeth (6–8)
Gastrointestinal	bile secreted (3) rectum patent (3) pancreatic islands appear (3) fixation of duodenum and colon (4)
Respiratory	definitive shape of lungs (3) accessory nasal sinuses developing (4) elastic fibers appear in lung (4)
Urogenital	kidney able to secrete (2½) vagina regains lumen (5) testes descend into scrotum (7–9)
Vascular	definitive shape of heart (1½) heart becomes four-chambered (3½) blood formation in marrow begins (3) spleen acquires typical structure (7)
Nervous	commissures of brain complete (5) myelinization of cord begins (5) typical layers of cortex (6)
Special Senses	nasal septum complete (3) retinal layers complete, light-perceptive (7) vascular tunic of lens pronounced (7) eyelids open (7–8)

CHART 2-2

Biological and Psychological Behavior Observed from the 28th Week to Birth (Gesell, 1945)

28–32 Weeks

movements meager, fleeting, poorly sustained
lack of muscular tone
mild avoidance responses to bright light and sound
in prone position turns head to side
palmar stimulation elicits barely perceptible grasp
breathing shallow and irregular
sucking and swallowing present but lack endurance
no definite waking and sleeping pattern
cry may be absent or very weak
inconstant tonic neck reflex

32–36 Weeks

movements sustained and positive
muscle tone fair under stimulation
moro reflex present
strong but inadequate response to light and sound
in prone position turns head, elevates rump
definite periods of being awake
palmar stimulation causes good grasp
good hunger cry
fairly well-established tonic neck reflex

36–40 Weeks

movements active and sustained
muscle tone good
brief erratic following of objects with eyes
moro reflex strong
in prone position attempts to lift head
active resistance to head rotation
definite periods of alertness
cries well when hungry and disturbed
appears pleased when caressed
hands held as fists much of time, good grasp
tonic neck reflex more pronounced to one side (usually right) than to the other
good, strong sucking reflex

psychological factors (interaction of total organism with environmental events) of the uterine environment. This approach takes into consideration the effects of the genetic composition of the fetus which constantly interacts with other factors. Genetic influences are distinguished from other physical and chemical factors in that they operate solely from within the cells of the fetus itself.

To amplify this, we review some elementary but basic biology. At conception there comes into existence a new organism that will be similar in appearance and physiological functioning to all other members of the same species, and yet will be uniquely different from all others. The organism's potential for biological growth is in part dependent on the special composition of the substances transmitted in the parental sex cells and in part dependent upon subsequent environmental events, both inside and outside the new unit. Hereditary and environmental variables interact continuously throughout the life of the organism.

Heredity may be thought of as one of the sources of developmental causes. The genes, tiny units in the nucleus of the cell, are substances in the newly formed organism that have been transmitted, once and for all, through the parents' sex cells at the time of fertilization. The genes are not little models of later traits grown larger; they are more appropriately thought of as electrochemical processes which influence specific changes in development. Genes interact with one another and with other physical, chemical, and psychological variables to produce organismic structures and their functionings. "The operation of heredity in bringing about development of a living individual occurs by means of assimilation of food and of growth. . . . Heredity furnishes the pattern of these transformations, which build a likeness of the assimilating body out of the materials taken from the environment" (Dobzhansky, 1960).

The kind and amount of these materials and the times at which they are provided influence variations in the otherwise inherited "likeness" of this assimilating body.

Environment may also be thought of as another source of variables affecting development. The interaction of environmental variables with hereditary variables starts at the moment of fertilization and continues relentlessly until the end of life. Dobzhansky (1956) summarizes the dynamics of growth in these words: "The interaction of heredity and environment makes the development of the organism pass through a succession of stages, from fertilization, through growth, reproduction, and old age, to death. At any stage the outcome of the development depends on the genotype and on the succession of environments which the developing organism has encountered up to that stage."

All too often heredity and environment have been thought of as separate and opposing forces, and questions have been raised about the relative importance of each in determining traits ranging from hair color to intelligence. Modern conceptions of both heredity and environment preclude this unrealistic oversimplified conception. The kinds of questions which now seem appropriate, in the sense of being answerable, probe into the possibility of producing both biological and psychological changes by manipulating either or both the genetic and environmental variables in specific ways and at specific times in development.

The following quotation from Arey (1954) serves well as a summary of our discussion thus far as to the relationship of hereditary and environmental variables:

> Heredity operates through internal factors, present in the fertilized egg itself. Chief among these are the *genes*, or the hereditary determiners which are located in the chromosomes of the nucleus; they are contributed equally to the fertilized egg by each parent. These genes are seen to act like enzymic catalyzing agents in directing the production of the special characteristics of the individual. It is suspected that the cytoplasm of the developing egg may be influential in establishing the more general characteristics that mark an individual as a human, a primate, a mammal, and a vertebrate. . . . Environment supplies the *external factors* that make development possible and allow heredity to find expression. Such environmental factors include light, temperature, moisture, food and various non-nutritive chemical substances. Both the external and the internal factors are components of a common system, and to weigh the value of one against the other is to lose sight of the integrated processes of development as a whole. Each is essential and important; all the developmental effects are produced co-operatively by interaction between genetic and environmental factors (pp. 6–7).

In order to determine the effect of genetic variables it would be necessary to manipulate the gene composition of the sex cells before fertilization, and then to observe the effect on development after fertilization. At the same time it would be necessary to control environmental conditions during the period of experimentation. This is what is usually done in an elementary experimental breeding study. The genes are "manipulated" by choosing the parents of the fetus according to their observable traits or behaviors (known or thought to be inherited). Environment is held "constant" by duplicating as nearly as possible the conditions under which parent-offspring development takes place and observing whether the predicted characteristics do indeed occur. Such experimentation, of course, is conducted only with infra-human organisms, usually with species that reproduce at a rapid rate, making it possible for the experimenter to gather large amounts of data in a relatively short time. There have been no such studies with humans and therefore there are few data directly relevant to alteration of genetic variables in the human organism.

In order to determine the effects of environmental variables on the course of prenatal development, conditions in and about the preborn organism would have to be varied in a systematic fashion from the moment of fertilization to birth. This too, of course, is hardly possible with the human organism.

However, much is known about the effects of environmental variables through careful studies of those "accidents of nature." Some of the conditions and their effects on the development of the organism will be briefly noted. In each case, the effect on the developing organism depends on at least three factors: the intensity of the interacting condition, the time when it occurs, and the physical state of mother and embryo at that time.

The differential effects of one variable were presented to the general public with dramatic force when it was recently discovered that thalidomide, advanced as a tranquilizer, did not always work only in that way. In some instances babies died immediately at birth; in others, the babies lived but with varying degrees of physical deformity: some without legs or arms, some with nearly normal arms but misshapen legs, and still others with normal legs but stumplike arms.

Biological Factors

The developing organism is influenced by such biological factors as the quality of the fertilized ovum; its implantation in the uterine wall, and the formation of the structures that protect it. Montagu (1950) elaborates in this way:

> Differences in pressure *in utero*, whether induced through internal or external forces; differences in position, umbilical cord entanglements, and similar factors may more or less adversely affect the development of the organism. Deformity may be caused by faulty position, mechanical shaking, temperature changes; asymmetry of the head may be produced by pressure of the head downward upon the thorax. Wry neck (torticollis) has been observed, and pressure atrophy of the skin indicates the kind of continuous stimulation to which the fetus may be exposed (p. 157).

The composition and functioning of the mother's blood and endocrine systems are also biological factors that affect the development of the fetus. Pregnant women with hypertension tend to lose many more of their first babies than average, and the number increases as the blood pressure increases. The factor of Rh incompatibility between the mother's and the fetus's blood can produce similar effects. Information on the effects of endocrine imbalances is rather limited; it is known, however, that the fetus grows very rapidly in diabetic mothers, that the birth weights of babies whose mothers subsequently develop diabetes are greater than average, and that the mortality rates of fetuses and infants of diabetic mothers are extremely high.

Nutritional Effects

Maternal nutrition in the early stages of fetal growth seems to be an important factor in the production of certain physical abnormalities. Poor maternal diets often are found in conjunction with stillbirths and congenital defects, with small size and weight, and with difficult births (Thompson, 1946). Frequent illnesses of such babies are common during the first six postnatal months.

Diseases, Infections, and Drugs

Wasting diseases of the mother, which adversely affect the development of the fetus, include cancer, tuberculosis, and pellagra. Detrimental infectious diseases may involve syphilis, rubella (German measles), small-pox, chicken pox, and the like.

Congenital deafness has been traced to mothers' use of quinine for malaria during pregnancy, and to the use of morphine by mothers who were addicts. The use of thalidomide, as mentioned above, has led to a high rate of abortions, death of the infant immediately after birth, and a wide range of limb deformities.

Physical Actions

Included in physical agents that may alter the course of development are massive doses of X-rays during the first few months of pregnancy, and excessive pressure that might result from injurious accidents. The severity of the birth process as indicated by the length and difficulty of labor, presentation, forceps delivery, and the complications of primiparity may also play a part.

THE ONSET OF PSYCHOLOGICAL BEHAVIOR AND DEVELOPMENT

Before examining the question of the onset of psychological behavior and development, it is important to compare and contrast biological and psychological development. Biological development refers to orderly changes in structure (anatomy) and in functioning (physiology). The latter includes circulation, respiration, alimentation, metabolism, and neuromuscular activities.

In contrast, psychological development refers to progressive changes in the behavior of a biologically changing organism in relation to a succession of environmental events which, for the most part, are products of the culture. Progressive changes in behavior may take many forms simultaneously: (1) changes in terms of the *number of responses to the same object*. When presented with a cube, a young infant will most likely put it into his mouth. Later he may also throw it on the floor, put it in a box, and stack it on other cubes, etc. (2) Changes may be increases in the *length of the sequence of behavior* (chains) which defines the ultimate response. The tinkle of a bell may produce a turning of the infant's head toward the object. Later the same stimulus will bring about head turning, grasping, and bringing-to-the-mouth behavior. (3) Progressive changes may be increases in the *number of other re-*

sponses in operation at the same time. In the initial stages of walking, practically all of the child's responses are engaged. Later he walks with ease and at the same time talks and uses his hands effectively to do other things, as in fielding a baseball. (4) Developmental behavior changes also include *increases in skill* (shaping of the topography) in any of the behaviors described above. Compare, for example, the awkward gait of a two-year-old and the smooth strides of a six-year-old.

The evolution of psychological equipment makes possible responding to new stimuli (brought about through the lowering of sensory thresholds like pain, for example), to gross differences between stimuli (tables and chairs, and humans and infrahumans), to subtle similarities and differences between stimuli (cats and dogs), and to more and more complex patterns arranged temporally (musical notes) or simultaneously (activities of guests at a birthday party). In other words the development of psychological equipment makes it possible for the individual to respond to stimuli with increased range and complexity.

Clearly, biological activity begins at the moment the individual begins: at fertilization. It is also true that psychological behavior starts prior to birth. But, at what point? This question has been of perpetual concern to psychologists. Answers to it, however, have been complicated by the intrusion of other considerations. One of these refers to the classical problem of the relationship between activation of the sensory organs and the beginnings of conscious experience. Another concerns the starting point of central nervous system functioning. Carmichael (1951), for example, says:

> Ordinarily the beginning of behavior, and hence the starting point of behavioral psychology, is placed at the point where true receptor-initiated neuromuscular activity begins. It is assumed that this point is the one at which activities of the organism take place which involve sense organs and nervous system as well as muscles (p. 62).

Rather than attempting to establish the onset of psychological behavior in terms of inferences about the beginning of conscious experience, or the initial activation of the central nervous system, it is suggested that in keeping with the definitions advanced to this point, we look to data suggesting first indications that the organism reacts to environmental events in a *unified* manner.

Even when cast solely in functional terms, the determination of the beginning of psychological interaction is still a knotty problem. A lack of methodological technique limits the availability of valid and reliable data. As has been pointed out, generalizing current findings to normal fetal development is questionable since:

1. Most of the data are from observations on fetuses removed from the uterus, often under circumstances of fetal anoxia, release from normal pressures exerted in amniotic sac, breakdown in temperature control, and the administration of anesthetic drugs to the mother.
2. Different investigators have used different methods to stimulate and observe fetal behavior. Their equivalence or non-equivalence needs to be evaluated since it is axiomatic in scientific analysis that what is observed is in some part changed by the method of making the observation.
3. Techniques have not as yet been developed to ascertain with accuracy some of the basic parameters of the fetus, such as age, or time from fertilization to time of observation.

Current findings may soon be revised and augmented by new technologies. Many of these are, curiously, by-products of research in space exploration. For example, telemetric instrumentation devices (which do not require connecting wires) could allow continuous observation of fetal activities *in utero* without interfering with or disturbing the fetus's normal course of development.

In any case, available data from a variety of sources suggest that the fetus can respond as a unified system at about 24 weeks of age. At this time the fetus is capable of lung breathing and of producing a thin, crying noise in case of premature birth. In order to be certain that the organism is definitely functioning as a total system, however, we would be safer to consider 28 weeks as a more reasonable starting point of psychological interaction. As shown in Chart 2-2, the fetus at this time is capable of (1) meager, fleeting, and briefly sustained movements with poor muscular tonicity, (2) mild avoidance responses to bright light and sound, (3) turning the head to the side when in prone position, (4) a barely perceptible grasp response to palmar stimulation, (5) weak sucking and swallowing behavior, (6) weak crying, and (7) an inconstant tonic neck reflex (Gesell, 1945). In addition, the organism's nervous, circulatory, and other systems are developed well enough to function adequately in case of premature birth. Because of this criterion, 28 weeks is often referred to as the minimal age of viability.

THE NATURE OF PRENATAL PSYCHOLOGICAL BEHAVIOR

It will be recalled that the probability of a response under specified conditions is a function of events occurring at the moment of observation and the interactional history of the individual with respect to similar situations. Hence, knowledge of psychological events from their inceptions is essential for the complete analysis of behavior at any point in the developmental continuum, before or after birth. Unfortunately, as indicated above, there are few data on the kinds and amounts of psychological activities that take place *in utero,* largely because of the relative inaccessibility of these interactions for observation.

What is known about prenatal psychological activity and the consequences to the infant at the time of birth? Munn (1955) gives a commonsense account of what might happen *in utero:* "After the organism attains a certain degree of motility it is, of course, able to stimulate itself. Movements of the trunk and limbs not only cause movements of the amniotic fluid and consequent tactile stimulation, but lead to proprioceptive stimulation of neighboring regions. There are possibilities, also, of direct tactile stimulation of parts of the body by the hands and feet" (p. 188).

Holt (1931) and others have suggested that behavior at birth is determined, to a considerable extent, by prenatal psychological activity. It is conceivable that part of the changes that come about would do so through respondent processes. Let us consider some of the research which attempts to evaluate respondent processes in the fetus.

It is accepted as fact that the fetus *in utero* reacts with gross movement to sound stimuli of considerable intensity during the last few months of gestation (e.g., Bernard & Sontag, 1947). Several investigators, such as Ray (1932), have attempted to use this fact to see whether gross movements so aroused can be conditioned to another stimulus. Their findings failed to produce clear-cut evidence. Spelt (1948), however, using improved techniques, claimed that the human fetus can be conditioned experimentally during the last months of pregnancy. Because of the discrepancy between Spelt's findings and those previously reported, Spelt's study will be described in some detail before evaluating his conclusion.

The eliciting stimulus (unconditioned stimulus) was a loud noise produced by a large clapper striking a box. The stimulus to be conditioned (or neutral stimulus) was a vibratory stimulus produced by a doorbell modified and arranged to vibrate perpendicularly to the surface of any part of the abdomen. The response (fetal movement) was recorded by three tambours (cups with rubber covers highly sensitive to slight variations in pressure) taped to the mother's abdomen. Two classes of responses from the mother were also recorded: her breathing rate and the indications that she felt fetal movement.

The subjects were 13 obstetric patients, and three non-pregnant women, in whom the conditioning should fail. Eleven of the 13 obstetric patients were past seven months of pregnancy. The 16 subjects were studied as follows:

Group I. This was the experimental group. It consisted of five pregnant women who were given a series of conditioning trials involving the pairing of the two stimuli, with the vibratory stimulus preceding the noise stimulus by five seconds. These pairings were repeated every four minutes or so.

Prior to this conditioning sequence, three of the women were tested to see whether the loud noise (unconditioned stimulus) sensitized rather than conditioned the fetus to the vibration (conditioned stimulus). Accordingly, the loud noise and vibrations were not paired; they were both presented but at different times. There was a series of eight to 16 loud noise presentations followed by a series of three to 10 vibrations presentations. The findings were negative: reactions to loud noises did not result in reactions to vibration stimulations.

The other two pregnant women were given five to 15 vibrations *without* prior stimulation by the loud noise to see whether the vibrations alone would produce fetal movement, without benefit of conditioning. Again the findings were negative: vibrations alone did not produce fetal movements.

The conditioning procedures produced successive responses to the conditioned stimulus with varying degrees. For example, two subjects showed three successive responses by the eighth session at which time the experiment was terminated because of the onset of labor, one produced seven successive conditioned responses in the sixth session, and one showed two successive conditioned responses in the seventh session followed by three more at the beginning of the ninth. Continued presentation of the conditioned stimulus after conditioning resulted in no responding in three subjects. After four successive conditioned stimuli produced no response a series of successive conditioned responses occurred after a 24-hour rest period in one subject.

Groups II, III, and IV. These served as control groups. Group II consisted of six women, all in the late eighth or the ninth month of pregnancy. They were given the conditioned stimulus alone to see whether this stimulus became effective simply as the result of advancing fetal maturity. No responses to the vibrations were observed under this condition.

Group III consisted of three non-pregnant women. They were given the regular conditioning procedures. The findings were also negative, as they should have been; no conditioning was observed. This suggests that the responses recorded were produced by the fetus rather than by the woman.

Group IV consisted of two pregnant women with whom the effect of fetal age on the response to sound alone was investigated by beginning presentation in the seventh month of gestation. Findings indicated that the unconditioned stimulus was ineffective before the eighth calendar month.

The general conclusions were: (1) conditioning, extinction, and spontaneous recovery were demonstrated; (2) the loud noise was ineffective before the eighth month of pregnancy; (3) the results were not confounded with maternal movements; and (4) the correlation between maternal signals of fetal movement and movements shown on objective records was high (p. 78).

Despite the care with which this study was conducted, interpretations should be made with caution. First, the study has not yet been repeated. In other words, the reliability of the findings has not as yet been supported by replication. Second, studies attempting to show stable conditioning in the neonate have not produced clear-cut results. It would seem that studies of the neonate should give at least as clear-cut results as this one on the fetus, not only because of the advanced development of the former but also because more direct methods of stimulating and recording are possible. Third, the movement responses of the fetus recorded may have been uterine contractions of the pregnant mother rather than gross motor activities of the fetus. (A nonpregnant woman might not show such responses.) Fourth, the sensitization procedures applied to the first three women may have been short. More presentation of loud noise alone might have resulted in producing responses to the vibratory stimulus. It will be recalled that eight to 16 loud noise presentations were given to see whether sensitization to vibratory stimuli alone could be demonstrated. At least 15 to 20 presentations should have been given, since these were the minimum number said to be necessary to produce conditioned responses. Fifth, as Lipsitt (1963) points out, the mother may have been reacting to the unconditioned stimulus (loud sound). It would be advantageous in future studies of this sort to have the mother subjected to continuous masking sound through earphones while the unconditioned stimulus is delivered.

The only firm conclusion at present is that the possibility of fetal conditioning should be left open until more data become available. The results of future studies exploiting new techniques for presenting stimuli and recording reactions should prove especially valuable. We also need studies designed to control for conditionable, painless, uterine maternal contractions occurring between the seventh and ninth months of pregnancy.

If the possibility of respondent conditioning in the fetus is dubious, then any prospects for operant conditioning at that stage of development are indeed fanciful. There may well be a time late in gestation when the fetus is well enough organized as an integral organism to be susceptible to reinforcement contingencies, but what these contingencies might be remains entirely a matter of speculation. The fetus is well maintained with the necessities of life by the mother's physiology and is well insulated from many of the stimuli which will function as reinforcers for him after birth.

A number of substances can pass the placental barrier between child and mother, and some of these, conceivably, could function as a reinforcing stimulus. Adrenalin might be one such example. Even if it did have a reinforcing function, it is not clear that it would enter into contingencies with the fetus's behavior and serve to strengthen or weaken that behavior. The position of the fetus within the uterus conceivably could apply pressures to him in ways that could be negatively reinforcing; perhaps some global responses of his body might shift him into a better position which relieved these pressures. It is clear that late in gestation the fetus moves often, but nothing is known about the stimulus functions of the consequences of such movements. In short, it is imaginable that reinforcement contingencies operate during prenatal life to strengthen operant behaviors in rough ways, but there is no evidence to support such speculation.

BIRTH—A SALTATORY ENVIRONMENTAL EVENT

Birth has been fancifully thought of, at one extreme, as a time when the fetus is dispossessed from its "uterine paradise"; at the other, as the moment when it is released from almost unbearable restriction. It will never be known whether the fetus views his own birth as a disturbing intrusion of his complacency or as a long-awaited leap into freedom. What will probably be known is more about the physiological and behavioral effects of a saltatory transformation from the uterine to the external environment.

Let us define our terms. The uterine environment may be analyzed as a set of variables emanating from the biological functioning of the mother, events from the biological functioning of the fetus, and the external physical environment acting through the body of the mother. The external environment (the environment outside of the uterus) may be viewed as consisting of physical conditions acting directly on the organism, social conditions (especially the behavior of parents and caretakers), and events from the biological functioning of the individual. In addition the uterine environment provides the organism with an aquatic medium, while the post-birth environment provides him with an atmospheric medium. This difference should not be overlooked, since stimuli and responses have differential effects under each medium condition.

Three consequences of birth will be discussed in the context of their possible functions for the infant's behavior: (1) the drastic changes that take place in biological interactions, (2) the changes in the composition of the external environment, and (3) the probable damaging effects on the organism of the birth process.

Changes in Biological Interactions

When it is said that birth brings about drastic biological changes, what is meant is at least that there is a change from a parasitic to an independent existence. In its parasitic existence the fetus is dependent upon the mother for respiration, digestion of food and the preparation of nutrient materials, excretory functions, thermal regulation, and protection from aversive stimuli. During the birth process the circulatory relations with the mother are terminated; autonomous respiration must commence or the neonate will be asphyxiated.

It is not clear what constitutes the necessary conditions for respiratory action to begin. Some investigators believe that it is started by cutaneous stimuli (tactual and thermal) which serve to bring about an enervation of the musculature of the thorax, while atmospheric pressure inflates the lungs. Others suggest that the essential condition is a critical concentration of CO_2 in the bloodstream of the neonate. Still others assert that the crucial conditions may involve both cutaneous stimulation and a certain concentration of CO_2 in the blood.

The interruption and cessation of circulatory relations with the mother also means that nutrient materials ready for assimilation are no longer available to the neonate. It must take food, digest it, and excrete it. Furthermore it must maintain a relatively uniform body temperature despite variations in the thermal environment. It is apparent that the birth process initiates many new forms of respondent behavior which serve these functions.

Changes in the Composition of Environmental Events

Clearly, birth makes it possible for new stimulus-response relationships to take place. Before birth, the amount, magnitude, and variety of stimuli interacting with the eyes, ears, nose, tongue, skin, and vestibular mechanism are quite limited. Those that do interact must possess certain properties to be effective through the amniotic fluid. Also, responses that act on the external environment, such as the movement of the head, torso, legs, and arms, are restricted and modified in their action by the position of the fetus, the limited space in the uterine cavity, and the liquid medium.

Damage Through Physical Action

The birth process may affect the anatomical structure and physiological functioning of the organism through direct mechanical action. Pressures during birth sometimes give rise to fractures of bones during passage from the birth canal, but the more common consequences are hemorrhages. They may be of slight extent and quickly absorbed; they may involve vital nerve centers and result in death; they may permanently affect part of the nervous system, with consequent impairment of function; or they may have both transitory and permanent consequences on such sense organs as the eye and the ear.

Some writers in the psychoanalytic tradition claim that there is also the possibility of "psychic" damage. They argue that a primal anxiety state, from which all subsequent anxiety states stem, has its origin in the birth process. Yet, clinical findings show that individuals delivered by Caesarean section, and who thereby avoid birth trauma, do not as adults seem to differ temperamentally from persons who have been delivered in the normal manner.

A study by Weil and Davis (1941) compared 500 children born naturally and those born with the aid of instruments. (If there were validity to the notion of psychological birth trauma, children born with the aid of instruments would be expected to show greater disturbance than those who were not.) Three hundred and eighty were born spontaneously and 120 were born with the aid of instruments. The investigators checked problem areas such as intelligence, overly submissive or aggressive behaviors, general hyperactivity, tics, school difficulties, intersibling conflicts, and physical ills. There were no differences in IQ between the two groups. The misbehaviors were generally more frequent in the "nontraumatic" spontaneous birth group! Thus, the available evidence, such as it is, does not support the concept of "psychic" birth trauma. Indeed, there is little need to postulate a "source" of anxiety, primal or otherwise. It is quite satisfactory to accept human behavior as it exists, which includes tendencies to escape and avoid aversive stimuli.

REFERENCES

Arey, L. *Developmental anatomy: a textbook and laboratory manual of embryology.* (6th ed.) New York: Sanders, 1954.

Bernard, J., & Sontag, L. W. Fetal reactivity and sound. *J. genet. Psychol.,* 1947, *70,* 205–210.

Carmichael, L. Ontogenetic development. In S. S. Stevens (Ed.), *Handbook of experimental psychology.* New York: Wiley, 1951.

Dobzhanski, T. *The biological basis of human freedom.* New York: Columbia University Press, 1960.

Gesell, A. The ontogenesis of infant behavior. In L. Carmichael (Ed.), *Manual of child psychology.* (2nd ed.) New York: Wiley, 1954.

Holt, E. B. *Animal drive and the learning process.* New York: Holt, 1931.

Hooker, D. *The prenatal origin of behavior.* Lawrence, Kans.: Univ. of Kansas Press, 1952.

Kantor, J. R. *Interbehavioral psychology.* (Rev. ed.) Bloomington, Ind.: Principia Press, 1959.

Lipsitt, L. P. Learning in the first year of life. In L. P. Lipsitt & C. C. Spiker (Eds.), *Advances in child development and behavior.* Vol. I. New York: Academic Press, 1963.

Montagu, M. F. A. Constitutional and prenatal factors in infant and child health. In M. J. E. Senn (Ed.), *Symposium on the healthy personality.* New York: Josiah Macy Jr. Found., 1950.

Munn, N. L. *The evolution and growth of human behavior.* Boston: Houghton Mifflin, 1955.

Ray, W. S. A preliminary report of a study on fetal conditioning. *Child Develpm.,* 1932, *3,* 175–177.

Spelt, D. K. The conditioning of the human fetus in utero. *J. exp. Psychol.,* 1948, *38,* 338–346.

Thompson, Helen. Physical growth. In L. Carmichael (Ed.), *Manual of child psychology.* (2nd ed.) New York: Wiley, 1946.

3

Psychological Analysis of the Neonate

INTRODUCTION

"Neonate" is the term applied to the infant immediately after birth. This stage of development is described by Pratt (1954):

> It is a period of adjustment and perfection of newly acquired vegetative functions. It is marked by the obsolescence of such structures as the ductus Botalli and the umbilical vein, and by the recovery from injuries such as asphyxia, umbilical infections, tetanus, obstetrical paralysis, and hemorrhages incurred during the birth process. It is likewise a period during which certain sensory-motor structures are first activated by adequate stimuli . . . (p. 217).

The length of the neonatal period varies with the purposes of the investigator. For present purposes, let us say it extends from birth at full term to the end of the second week. This span would allow an account of the psychological equipment of the neonate after most of the normal effects of birth had subsided, but prior to the acquisition of much of the behavior related to the postnatal environment.

The physical appearance of the average American neonate may be described as follows. The skin is red, blotched, and wrinkled, but within a few weeks will be smooth and pale. The average weight is about 7½ pounds, ranging from three to 16 pounds, with boys slightly heavier than girls. The average length of the neonate is 19½ inches, ranging roughly from 17 to 21 inches, with boys slightly longer than girls. The head is relatively large compared to the proportions in the adult. (The head of the neonate makes up about one quarter of the whole body; the adult's is about one seventh.) The amount of hair present can vary from none at all to a thick shock. The legs are bowed and are disproportionately short and thick, and the arms are short and thin. The shoulders are narrow, and the abdomen is relatively large and protruding. Ordinarily there is little neck at birth. The bones and muscles are soft. The limbs are uncontrolled. Eye focus may be uncoordinated. For some babies the eyes remain closed for several days. The mouth cavity is shallow, the roof being flat rather than concave like the adult's. Most neonates do not have teeth.

The physiology and anatomical structure of the neonate are not only interesting from the biological standpoint, but also from the psychological standpoint. These factors play a part in determining the onset and maintenance of much of the behavior of the individual. For example, it is obvious that the social community is more attentive and reactive to the cute, active, perceptive baby and less attentive and even evasive with respect to the unattractive, passive, and dull infant.

Most internal physiological functioning starts either during the fetal period or immediately after the birth cry. Included here are the circulatory, respiratory, endocrine, alimentary, and metabolic systems. The processes for regulating sleeping and dozing cycles are also in full operation.

RESPONDENT INTERACTIONS

The following rather extensive range of behavior is from a tabulation made by Dennis in 1934. It will be noted that in many instances, the independent stimulus conditions are not given. They are not yet identified. Dennis made an interesting comment on our state of knowledge regarding neonatal behavior in 1934:

> . . . while the literature on the newborn is large, it is relatively weak in naturalistic description and in interest and familiarity on the part of the experimenter with the material directly at hand. In most cases the observer has been looking for evidences of receptor or neurological function, or for adult or pathological parallels. A more direct approach may add greatly to the information which has just been summarized (p. 19).

CHART 3-1

Behavior of the Neonate

After each response are listed the stimulus procedures eliciting it, or the other behaviors correlated with it.

Eyelid Responses

opening—correlated with other activity
closing—touching the eye, lid, lashes, forehead, nose, cheeks, mucous membrane of the nose, sound, strong odors, bitter tastes, strong light, correlated with crying and sneezing

Pupillary Responses

dilation to weak light
constriction to strong light
widen to strong stimulation of the skin

Ocular Responses

pursuit
saccadic (fast lateral motions of very small sweep, maintaining constantly wavering image on retina; stabilization of image produces fading of image in adults)
nystagmus—cold (20° C.), rotation of body
coordinated compensatory eye movements—correlated with infant's own head movements, or with sharp jerks of head by the investigator
unspecific movements, random

Face and Mouth Responses

opening—touch stimuli around mouth
closing—touch stimuli around mouth
sucking—tongue and jaw motions—tactual and taste stimuli; hunger (?)
grimacing, twisting of face and mouth—bitter, salt, sour tastes, pricking of nose
yawning
tongue pushing—bitter, salt, sour tastes rejected
licking
lip pursing—touching about mouth
sneezing—smells of ammonia

CHART 3-1 *Continued*

Face and Mouth Responses Continued

coughing
gagging–tongue stimulation, bitter tastes
swallowing
hiccoughing
vomiting

Head Responses

dorsal (drawing back of head)–nose-holding, strong odors, bright light
ventral–less
turning–tactual stimuli to face or nose, touch on cheek, bright light away, weak light toward; turning of rest of body produces similar turn of head
head shudder–bitter tastes
head balancing–within few days

Hand and Arm Responses

radius reflex
scapulo-humeral reflex
handcloses–tactual stimulation to fingers or palm
flexion (withdrawal)–sharp tap or pinprick to hand
face rubbing–tickling stimuli to face, irritation of mucous membrane of nose, strong odors
random movements
startle (outward flinging of hands and arms)–sudden strong stimulation

Trunk Responses

back arching–nose pinching, being held upside down, crying, any stimulus producing dorsal head response
twisting–trunk twists in same direction as head is rotated by the investigator. If chest held, pelvis twists in opposite direction as head, squirming, in effect.
abdominal reflex

Sexual Responses

raising of testes–tactual stimulation of inner thigh
erection of penis (?)

CHART 3-1 *Continued*

Foot and Leg Responses

knee-jerk reflex
Achilles tendon reflex
flexion of leg—needle prick to foot or leg, pushing head down toward chest
extension of leg—gentle push (where?) sometimes strong enough to support baby's weight
kicking—free foot kicks at other when other is restrained, leg is pinched
inside knee—kicking with both legs usually alternating; correlates with crying
stepping—when held upright, feet touching surface

Coordinated Responses

resting, sleeping position—legs flexed, upper arms straight out from shoulders, forearms flexed to lie parallel with head, fists closed
opisthotonic position—back arch dorsally, head to heels (more extreme form of head rearing)
backbone reflex—concave bending of side of body which is tickled, stroked; leg on stroked side extends, contralateral leg flexes
lifting head and rump—if held horizontally in the air, when head is raised, rump raises too
"fencing"—when head is turned, faced arm extends, other flexes, faced leg extends, other flexes
"springing"—if held upright, inclined slightly forward, arms extend and legs are flexed
stretching—back arches, head arches back, legs extend, arms extend over head
startle response—head thrown back, arms thrown apart from body, fingers extend and fan out, legs extend, crying in extreme cases, sudden loud noises, falling, sudden touches, sudden widespread changes in temperature over surfaces of body, sudden blow to chest or abdomen, and also at random moments in absence of any obvious stimulus
creeping—in prone position, arms and legs drawn in under body, head lifted; feet may push against traction, and arms will move too
shivering, trembling, during urination

Despite lack of focus on the problem of interaction and the obscurity of many of the controlling stimuli, it is expected that in the future there will be more information on the relevant stimuli, since the grist for the mill of a functional analysis is knowledge of stimulus-response relationships. The psychological relevance of the "motor activity" or the "sensory capacity" of the neonate is essentially knowledge of the stimuli for the former and the responses produced by the latter. Changes in motor activities do not transpire independent of adequate stimulation, and sensory abilities are knowable only through discernible and reliable changes in responses—general or specific, smooth or striped.

Following is a list of respondents, emphasizing the *stimulus* aspects of the interactions. It is convenient to divide them in two parts—stimuli functionally antecedent to (1) biological behavior and (2) psychological behavior.

Biological Behavior (Reflexes)

Biological reflexes are those respondents which are not conditionable—no amount of pairing of neutral stimuli with the eliciting stimulus will bring the response under the control of the neutral stimulus alone. Biological reflexes (sometimes referred to as neurological reflexes) are usually evaluated in neurological examinations, and their presence or absence is thought to be related to the health or soundness of the nervous system.

Examples of biological reflexes which ordinarily remain throughout the lifetime of an individual are:

1. The patellar tendon reflex—a "kick" of the leg in response to a tap on the patellar tendon.
2. The biceps reflex—contraction of the biceps in response to a tap on the bicep tendon.
3. Triceps reflex—contraction of the triceps in response to a tap on the tricep tendon.
4. Abdominal reflex—contraction of the muscles around the umbilicus in response to a sharp downward stroke on the abdominal wall.
5. Achilles reflex—contraction of the foot muscle in response to a tap on the Achilles tendon.

Examples of biological reflexes which ordinarily "disappear" with maturity are:

1. Darwinian reflex—grasping an object that is placed in the palm. This reflex is no longer seen after about three months.
2. Babinski reflex—fanning and extension of the toes in response to gentle stroking of the sole of the foot. It is no longer seen after about six months.
3. Moro reflex—general "fear reaction" including embracing behavior in response to sudden and intense stimuli. The embracing part of the response pattern is practically eliminated at about seven months.

Psychological Behavior

Reference here is to diffuse behavior changes brought about by antecedent external stimulation. These interactions are classified as psychological because they involve relationships between a total functioning organism and environmental events and because they can be shown to be modifiable.

Interactions of this sort are usually studied in laboratories with automated devices for presenting experimental stimuli and for recording responses. Responses are recorded typically by means of a stabilimeter, which is a specially mounted bassinet designed to produce objective, graphic accounts of the bodily movements of an infant (Crowell, Peterson, & Safely, 1960; Lipsitt & DeLucia, 1960). Frequently measures of physiological functioning are also taken, such as heart rate, respiration rate, electroencephalograms, and galvanic (electrical) skin reactions.

Reactions to light. Infants usually show differential reactions to visual stimuli. "Intense light of short duration typically evokes a shift in the patterns of circulation and respiration; it may also elicit eyelid, ocular, ocular-neck reflex, and probably the Moro and startle responses. When stimulated with a flash of bright light the newborn shows, with some variability, a closing, or twitching of closed eyelids" (Pratt, Nelson, & Sun, 1930). "When a flash of intense light is thrown suddenly on the newborn's face, it evokes a more severe response when the infant is asleep than when awake" (Bryan, 1930).

Infants will also fixate on and orient to a source of light of moderate intensity and will follow, in an inaccurate fashion, a moving object. Nystagmus (a rapid involuntary oscillation of the eyeballs) is also evidenced. In later development visual pursuit successively displays fixation, horizontal following, vertical following, and circular following (Jones, 1926; Morgan & Morgan, 1944).

It is not clear whether neonates can discriminate color. There are, however, some recent data suggesting that they can react differentially to patterns (Fantz, 1963).

Reactions to sound. Most infants are sensitive to auditory stimulation over a range of loudness and duration. General bodily movements of a neonate increase irregularly with increases in sound intensities ranging from 30 to 85 decibels above the threshold of hearing of normal adults. Eyelid reflexes and circulatory and respiratory changes may also be involved (Haller, 1932; Stubbs, 1934).

Intense, high-pitched auditory stimuli that appear suddenly are most effective in arousing responses, and in many instances lead to startle, increased activity, and crying (Pratt, Nelson, & Sun, 1930).

As the duration of auditory stimuli increases, activity levels and breathing rate increase, and breathing becomes more shallow. This finding is based on the work of Stubbs (1934), who contrasted 1-, 3-, and 5-second durations with 15-second periods.

Reactions to stimuli on the tongue. Reactions to solutions on the tongue are not highly developed in the newborn. The general finding is that the neonate responds with sucking behavior and relaxed musculature following the admission of sweet solutions, and with grimaces and slight circulatory and respiratory changes to bitter solutions (quinine) most of the time (Pratt, Nelson, & Sun, 1930). Also, salt solutions tend to disrupt sucking behavior, while sugar solutions tend to maintain it.

> In general, respiration and circulation are least influenced by "sweet," slightly disturbed by "salt," and considerably affected by "sour" and "bitter" solutions. Sucking mounts with age to sugar solutions as do facial responses to quinine. There is some evidence that, beyond the threshold point, responses may be altered by differences in concentration of the taste solution (Pratt, 1954, pp. 243–244).

More definitive information on gustatory sensitivities of the neonate will undoubtedly be forthcoming when investigators begin to apply more recently developed techniques.

Reactions to odors. Strong gaseous stimuli (strong stimuli are required since the neonate does not respond to weaker, more subtle magnitudes) such as ammonia, oil of cloves, anise oil, acetic acid, violet perfume, turpentine, and asafoetida, will usually produce squirming, sneezing, grimacing, crying, turning, throwing back the head, and changes in respiration and circulation. In general these activities increase when the odors are more intense (Pratt, Nelson, & Sun, 1930; Disher, 1934).

Recently Engen, Lipsitt, and Kaye (1963) found that the greatest number of responses were elicited by acetic acid, with asafoetida next, followed by phenylethyl alcohol and anise oil. They noted, as did other investigators, that a marked decrease in responses was apparent as a function of repeated stimulation. This is the phenomenon of *adaptation,* which is one of the most commonly noted observations in virtually all investigations of relationships between stimuli and responses in the neonate. For example, several papers have been published on adaptation involving auditory (e.g., Keen, 1964) and electrotactual stimuli, and theoretical problems associated with this process have been discussed by Lipsitt (1963).

Reactions to temperature changes. The newborn infant responds to differences in the temperature of a liquid or a substance applied in the mouth or on the body. The thermal sensitivity of neonates to milk has been evaluated by observing changes in sucking behavior (Jensen, 1932). The range of individual differences to warm milk varied from 50 to 85 degrees centigrade, and for cold solutions, from five to 32 degrees centigrade.

Sensitivity to temperature changes on the forehead and on the inside surface of the leg has been observed by applying a cylinder against the skin with an average temperature of 11.5 degrees centigrade. In general, applications of this degree of coldness to the head are followed by head movements, and to the legs by flexion or extension (Pratt, Nelson, & Sun, 1930).

Reactions to pin pricks and electrotactual stimuli. The newborn shows a definite reaction to needle pricks and electrotactual stimuli soon after birth, and his sensitivity increases rapidly over the first three or four days of life (Sherman & Sherman, 1929; Lipsitt & Levy, 1959). The region around the head is more reactive to pricking stimuli than that around the legs (Sherman & Sherman, 1929).

Reactions to body orientation and movement. In response to shifts in posture, rotation of the body, and falling through space, the neonate gives postural reactions and shows generalized postural adjustments.

CONDITIONING IN THE NEONATE

Can behaviors such as sucking, blinking, limb-withdrawal, respiration, crying, motility, galvanic skin response, and "fear" reactions be conditioned in the neonate? That is, will neutral stimuli such as mild intensities of visual, auditory, tactual, or vestibular stimuli, after pairings with appropriate unconditioned stimuli, later by themselves evoke any of the aforementioned responses in the infant within the first two weeks after birth?

The answer to this question is indeed interesting, and highly essential for a systematic analysis of human psychological development. If conditioning can be demonstrated at this time, it suggests that stimulus and response functions begin developing at least during the first weeks of postnatal life. Loosely stated, it means that the everyday stimuli in interaction with the neonate will begin to take on meanings for him.

As mentioned previously, if conditioning cannot be demonstrated in the neonate we should be extremely cautious in accepting findings purporting to show stable conditioning in the fetus during the last two months of gestation. Furthermore, if conditioning cannot be demonstrated in the first weeks of postnatal life, when may it be said to begin? We would also like to know the order in which topographically different responses may show conditioning properties (Is it easier to condition sucking or respiration?), and the order in which stimuli from different modalities may acquire conditioned functions (Is it easier to condition to visual or to tactual stimuli?).

Respondent

In the past a number of investigators have reported stable respondent conditioning in the neonate. Their studies have been criticized, however, for inadequate control of the effect of the conditioned and unconditioned stimuli, rapid maturational effects, and sampling error in the selection of subjects (Wickens & Wickens, 1940). Russian investigators have gone so far as to state that respondent conditioning in the neonate is impossible (Elkonin, 1957). They maintain, according to Brackbill (1960), that respondent conditioning of sucking, orienting behavior (head-turning and visual pursuit), or blinking may not reliably be demonstrated in the first two weeks, but requires about one month using a vestibular stimulus such as a change in body position. Only after about two months these responses are conditionable using an auditory (any complex tone), a tactile (brush against sole of foot), or an olfactory stimulus (oil of roses or lavender). At about two and one-half months they are conditionable with taste stimuli (5% sugar solution), and at about three months with visual stimuli (diffuse light).

Recently experimental child psychologists in this country have approached the problem of neonatal conditioning again, using more precise measuring and controlling techniques. For example, Crowell (1963) and Gullickson (1963) conducted extensive series of studies using electrotactual stimulation as an unconditioned stimulus for foot-withdrawal, and tone for a conditioned stimulus. Lipsitt and Marum (1960) worked comprehensively with the same set of variables. All had to conclude that with the variables described the question of stable conditioning in the neonate must still be left open.

Within the past year Lipsitt and Kaye (1964) approached the problem with a different unconditioned stimulus and response. A tone was used as a conditioning stimulus, or the neutral stimulus to be made into the conditioned stimulus, and insertion of a nipple in baby's mouth as the unconditioned stimulus to elicit sucking movements. One group of neonates received the tone paired with the insertion of the nipple, the other did not. Presence and number of sucking movements to the tone were recorded independently by two observers. On the average, sucking in response to the tone was greater in infants who received paired presentations of the tone and sucking device than in infants who received unpaired presentations of the same stimuli. These are encouraging findings; however, the issue is not closed. Further study is necessary to verify these results and to check and recheck on the possible influence of other variables.

Operant

We do not know whether operant conditioning can be demonstrated in the neonate. Data on the subject are meager. There is, however, a little information from studies concerned with problems centered around respondent conditioning, adaptation, and sensory thresholds. Let us consider what might be gleaned from some of these studies.

Dorothy Marquis (1931) performed a respondent conditioning experiment that might be interpreted as relevant to operant conditioning. She designed a study to "investigate the contention of the Pavlovian school of Russian psychologists and physiologists that the formation of conditioned responses in newborn infants is impossible because the cerebral cortex of the human infant functions only very incompletely the first few months after birth" (p. 208).

The unconditioned response was the feeding behavior of the infant (sucking, mouth-opening, and quieting, etc.) in response to milk from the nursing bottle. The stimulus to be conditioned to evoke the feeding behavior was a buzzer.

Basically, her procedure consisted of sounding the buzzer for five seconds, inserting the bottle in the infant's mouth, and sounding the buzzer again for five seconds after sucking had started. In addition, the buzzer was sounded for five seconds at various times while the infant was sucking. During each experimental session the bottle was removed from two to five times, and then replaced, preceded by the buzzer. This routine was followed for all six of the baby's daily feedings.

> Increase in mouth-opening and decrease in crying after the buzzer, in most infants, started on the fourth day, while increase in sucking and general activity began, in most instances, on the fifth day. With one exception, the seven infants who showed an increase in number of food-taking reactions *after* the buzzer, showed the least increase when they were quiet and asleep *before* the buzzer sounded (p. 483).

Marquis concluded that conditioning had been demonstrated in seven of the eight infants and that this was evidence bearing on the developmental status of the neonate's nervous system.

> Since present neurological evidence indicates that the cerebral cortex of the newborn infant functions only very incompletely the first few months after birth, we may infer that *conditioned responses can be formed in newborn infants, at least, by subcortical correlation.* The type of responses included in the conditioned foodtaking reactions to the buzzer indicates that the midbrain and especially the red nucleus was important as a controlling mechanism (p. 488).

Putting aside speculations about the parts of the brain which participate in the establishment of a classical conditioned response, it may be worthwhile to reexamine these procedures and findings in the context of operant conditioning. Marquis presented her neutral stimulus, the buzzer, for five seconds, then the nursing bottle, which carried tactual stimulation to the lips. The infant sucked and obtained milk while the buzzer was sounded for an additional five seconds. The buzzer was also sounded for five seconds every now and then while the infant was nursing. The buzzer and tactual lip stimulation were therefore present while sucking behavior was reinforced. Under these conditions the buzzer could have developed discriminative properties (as a cue for milk) and thereby acquired reinforcing properties.

Seven of the eight infants showed strong sucking, mouth-opening, and lip-pursing by the fifth day of the study. It is possible that these responses were under the control of the buzzer as a discriminative stimulus, or an eliciting stimulus, or both. It is interesting to note, however, that the average sucking curve for the seven infants begins to decline after day 7, for mouth-opening after day 6, and for combined sucking, mouth-opening, and lip-pursing after day 8. It is possible that these decrements were the beginning of the establishment of operant discrimination—the buzzer alone was losing its discriminative function (since it was not followed by milk), while the buzzer plus lip stimulation was being maintained.

Marquis conducted two control studies. In one she demonstrated that the infants who had been conditioned to a buzzer did not respond with sucking behavior when a flash light or a noise from the fall of a hammer striking a can was substituted for the buzzer: this shows that the infants were not made sensitive or reactive to stimulus change as such (at the intensity levels tested). In the other, performed on a new group of subjects, she demonstrated that infants do not ordinarily respond to a buzzer by sucking: this indicates that the buzzer was initially a neutral stimulus. However, she did not determine whether the sucking is controlled primarily by antecedent tactual stimulation on the lips and therefore eliciting *respondent* behavior, or by consequent stimuli (food in the mouth) and therefore *operant* behavior. There was no reason why she should. It must be remembered that this study was conducted 34 years ago; at that time most investigators assumed that all conditioning was respondent.

We turn now to a second study which may have implications for operant conditioning in the newborn. In this one, by Jensen (1932), most of the subjects were neonates (although a few were as old as three weeks). The natural sucking responses in feeding were recorded by an extremely sensitive method of recording pressure changes inside the nursing bottle. It was then possible to produce data showing the control over sucking behavior exercised by the taste and temperature of the fluid ingested.

Jensen's procedure was to establish a baseline of sucking behavior, using milk at 40 degrees centigrade, for ten seconds. (This is a short operant level, but one collected at repeated intervals. Data indicated that the response was sufficiently stable for this purpose.) The bottle was removed for 20 seconds and replaced for 20 seconds with another bottle holding the experimental mixture (milk or formula, sterile water, or various concentrations of salt or glucose), at the same or different temperatures. After a 20-second delay, the baseline was remeasured (milk at 40° C. was given), sometimes for 20 seconds. This sequence of base-line-delay-experimental mixture-day-baseline continued until six base-line periods had been recorded. The method was adequate to show differential sucking to variations in the temperature and taste of the experimental mixtures.

Since temperature and taste are stimulus consequences of the response, their control over sucking may testify to their reinforcing qualities and affect sucking as an operant. However, the stimuli are also immediate antecedents of the *next* response, given the usual rate of sucking. The control produced therefore may be related to their eliciting qualities in a respondent paradigm. These distinctions are, of course, absent from Jensen's report (the year was 1932).

Be it eliciting, discriminative, or reinforcing, the close stimulus control achieved is intriguing. Although it will not be easy to accomplish, experiments should be performed to establish whether sucking behavior is under the control of antecedent or consequent stimuli, or both.

It was pointed out earlier that incidental observations in investigations on other problems might shed light on the possibility of operant conditioning in the neonate. A study on olfactory stimulation by Engen, Lipsitt, and Kaye (1963) will serve as an example. These investigators found that following successive presentations of odor stimuli (mostly acetic acid, but also asafoetida), the neonate's response pattern changed progressively from a diffuse, seemingly disorganized response (similar to a mild startle) to a smooth, efficient response escaping the odor stimulus. In the early sessions the infant's entire body seemed to respond, while in later ones, a simple efficient and effective retraction or turn of the head from the locus of the stimulus was executed. This could be a combination of respondent conditioning and operant escape training (i.e., differentiation of an escape response). In regard to the latter, the head movement away from the source of the odor differentially reinforces that act by reducing the intensity of the stimuli. The other bodily responses were not so reinforced, and consequently weakened. Whether or not it is reasonable to say that such head-turning in the neonate is strengthened by consequent reduction of an aversive odor depends on data yet to be gathered.

One final point: a large component of the bodily activity or motility of a neonate is almost certainly operant in nature. It would be interesting to see what the outcome would be if an investigator made a record of the infant's behavior output over several sessions to obtain a baseline of his activity level, then systematically reinforced increases in activity with a stimulus demonstrated to be reinforcing for that infant. If the neonate's activity level reliably increased over baseline, there would be some reason to believe the consequent stimulus had some control over motility. This conclusion would have to be checked further, however, by withdrawing the contingency and observing that the activity level returned to baseline according to the laws of operant extinction. Reliable findings from such a study, together with those from investigations like Marquis's, Jensen's, and Engen, Lipsitt, and Kaye's, would have significant systematic and practical implications.

EMOTIONAL BEHAVIORS

Does the neonate have emotions? If so, what are they? These frequently asked questions cannot be answered without discussing the concept of emotion. Any such comments might well be introduced by a quotation from Woodworth & Schlosberg: "The topic of emotion has perhaps generated more unprofitable controversy among psychologists than any other with which they have concerned themselves. Yet it is by no means a topic which they can cast aside, for it covers a very important group of phenomena" (1954).

In an effort to avoid further "unprofitable controversy," "emotion" is viewed here as a general term referring to interactions between stimulating conditions and broad but definite patterns of certain respondent behaviors, possibly involving certain operant components (Vol. I, Chapter 6). The respondents of the neonate are extensive; the nameable operants may consist of only a few specific responses such as sucking and some general responses such as motility and gross body movements. Some of the respondents, such as crying, are traditionally called "emotional." Operants taking on shape in situations where "emotional" respondents are elicited often are tarred with the same brush. Thus, the "emotions" are behaviors arbitrarily singled out by verbal tradition; they have no other special status.

Emotions have been treated as relationships between objectively definable stimulating conditions and response patterns before, for example in 1919 by Watson. He claimed that the newborn has three unlearned emotions: love, fear, and anger; and that all the other emotions described in everyday conversation (delight, grief, sorrow, etc.) evolve through conditioning in the culture. He postulated that:

1. Love consists of a "cessation of crying, smiling, attempts at gurgling and cooing released by stimulation of some erogenous zone, tickling, shaking, gentle rocking, patting, and turning upon the stomach across the attendant's knee."
2. Fear consists of a "sudden catching of the breath, clutching randomly with the hands (the grasping reflex invariably appearing when the child is dropped), sudden closing of the eyelids, puckering of the lips, then crying." This pattern is released by sudden intense stimulation, loss of support, shaking or jarring.
3. Rage consists of crying, screaming, stiffening of the body, slashing or striking movements of the hands and arms, and holding the breath and flushing the face. These reactions are the consequences of hampering or restricting the infant's movements.

Since Watson's theory was stated in objective terms, definitive experimental tests were possible. Some were made; they did not support Watson's view. Three relatively invariant response patterns were not elicited by the three classes of stimuli described.

It seemed that (1) chain-breaking (specifically, interference in sucking behavior by withdrawal of nipple or depletion of milk before satiation), (2) sudden, intense, and long-enduring stimulus actions, and (3) prolonged deprivation of primary or homeostatic reinforcers could bring about simultaneously two classes of behavior change. One, frequently called the "activation" syndrome, is physiological in nature and includes increases in breathing, in heart rate, in adrenal gland activity, and in sweat gland functioning; decrease or cessation in smooth-muscle functioning; a dilation of the trondioles in the lungs and the pupils of the eyes; and a decrease in galvanic skin resistance.

The other class of reactions consists of rapid movements of the arms, legs, and head, and at times vigorous crying behavior. This class, together with the physiological reactions described above, is often called "distress."

While such interactions are taking place, it is apparent that the action of other stimuli with only mild to moderate intensities would not have their usual effects. For example, it is not likely that the neonate will track or "pay attention" to a glittering object moving across his visual field while reacting to strong tactile stimulation that could be produced by gastric pains.

There is a second class of interactions, often called "delight" or "relaxed state," that should be included in an analysis of emotional behavior. It is generated by the following:

1. Presenting mild and steady auditory and visual stimuli (Weiss, 1934).
2. Dressing with comfortable clothing (which may provide tactual and/or thermal stimuli) (Irwin & Weiss, 1934).
3. Holding and mild stroking of the skin (Crowell, 1963).
4. Presenting a reinforcer, especially after a period of considerable deprivation.

Under these circumstances autonomic physiological functioning is below normal, and arm, leg, and head movements are usually described as relaxed. Short bursts of sucking in response to a nipple are also observed now and again (Jensen, 1932).

Such interactions would, of course, not take place if the infant were long deprived of homeostatic stimuli or exposed to aversive stimulation. When the conditions are such that "relaxed" behavior does take place (e.g., satiation for food, ample sleep and rest, and moderate external temperature), reactions to other stimuli will not be likely unless they are of high intensities.

EFFECTS OF STIMULUS DEPRIVATION AND SATIATION AND OTHER SETTING EVENTS

It will be recalled that conditions which influence the strength of a stimulus-response relationship are called setting events. Examples are satiation and deprivation of homeostatic stimuli, the physical health of the child, the phase in the sleep-awake cycle, and the like. In making an inventory of the behavior equipment of the neonate, it is interesting to review what is known about behavior changes that seem to be related to setting events involving homeostatic conditions—deprivation of food and water, oxygen, sleep, activity, and the aftermath of aversive stimulation.

Food and Water

Food and water are considered together since they are usually given together in the form of milk or formula. Although there are wide individual differences, the neonate is typically least active immediately after feeding and most active immediately before feeding, and the closer in time to the next feeding, the greater the motility (Irwin, 1932). In general, he tends to be awake for a short time after feeding (this may be related to the activity involved in changing the infant after nursing), awake (and vocal) for a short time before the next feeding, and asleep during the middle part of the time between feedings.

Changes in the neonate's motility and internal functioning in the direction of the activation syndrome are correlated with increases in deprivations for food and water. Irwin (1932), for example, reports that food and water deprivation results in activity so great, even within normal feeding schedules, that it is prepotent with respect to the effects of ordinary auditory and visual stimuli.[1]

Sleep

There is no systematic information on the effects of sleep deprivation in the newborn. To obtain such data, the investigator would have to employ an objective criterion of degree of wakefulness and have control over the stimulating conditions that influence level of wakefulness. The method by which the infant is kept awake would be a condition that would have to be described and taken into account in analyzing the findings. (This again is a specific instance of the general research principle in the physical,

[1] The investigator studying the effects of external stimuli in the neonate has to be sure, therefore, that the effects of food and water deprivation are at a minimum and are maintained at a relatively constant level throughout his study.

biological, and behavioral sciences that whatever is observed is in part a function of the method of observing.)

The effects of loss of sleep may be complicated. For example, under natural circumstances, the neonate may be prevented from sleeping over prolonged periods because of illness or upsets of one sort or another. One cannot tell without careful and detailed analysis whether the behavior observed during such periods is due to sleep deprivation, aversive stimulation from the illness, or both.

In any event, the limited available information suggests that sleep deprivation increases the motility of the neonate and that after a certain period the activation syndrome would be observed. Deprivation of sleep would also be expected to be a condition which would reduce the effectiveness of stimuli operating over normal ranges.

Activity

Because of Watson's claim that in the neonate restraint of activity is necessary to elicit rage behavior, there has been considerable interest in the effect of preventing the neonate from engaging in normal striated-muscle activity (movements of the neck, arms, and legs). On the basis of a review of research, Dennis (1940) draws the conclusion that restraint of the neonate's movement without the use of intense stimulation (e.g., *forceful* holding) does not cause any intense activity reasonably described as "rage."

It is quite likely that the prevention of activity without aversive stimulation, as in swaddling, has a quiescent effect. Irwin and Weiss (1934), for example, observed the overt activity and amount of crying of newborns in both clothed and unclothed states. They found that (1) the neonates who were clothed were quieter and cried less than those who were unclothed, and (2) reduction in activity observed under clothed condition was maintained throughout the period of study.

Opportunity to Breathe

As would be expected, no information is available on the behavioral effects of systematic reductions of opportunities to breathe under laboratory conditions. Such information will never be obtained because of the possible detrimental consequences of such operations to the brain. Some light is thrown on the problem as it relates to anoxia in infrahuman studies (e.g., Meier, Bunch, Nolan, & Scheidler, 1960).

The Aftermath of Aversive Stimulation

It is clear that sudden, intense, and long-enduring stimulus actions bring about vast changes in smooth- and striped-muscle behaviors (recall the previous discussion of emotion). The term applied to this pattern of behavior change has been "excitement." Thus, strong aversive stimulation may be described as a setting event. The period following such aversive stimulation fits in well with this concept of a setting event, in that during this period the baby may be highly sensitive to certain classes of stimuli and highly insensitive to certain others, in contrast to normal times. After accidental exposure to a traumatizing auditory stimulus, it may be observed that for a while the baby shows startle responses or whimpers and cries in response to relatively mild stimuli. The baby seems to be sensitized to auditory stimuli. He may also show a lack of interest in relation to things that have in the past aroused looking and head-turning behavior. These types of interactions are the same phenomena that adults experience all too often—an emotional upheaval may be shown to decrease their work input and increase their tendency to engage in certain behaviors (ordinarily of low strength) such as sulking, complaining, or overeating.

CONTINUITY OF EMOTIONAL AND MOTIVATIONAL VARIABLES

It will be noted that deprivation and satiation for homeostatic stimuli are included under the concept of setting events, and extreme deprivation of homeostatic stimuli is included under circumstances producing the excitement type of emotional behavior. This apparent overlap in motivational and emotional interactions is resolved as follows: Deprivation over "ordinary ranges" has setting-events properties; at the extremes, it has both setting-events and emotionalizing properties.

Furthermore, different collections of setting events and emotional operations lead to similar reaction patterns in the neonate. On one hand, extensive deprivation of homeostatic stimuli and setting events of high intensities trigger the activation syndrome and heighten the overt activity level (including crying) to a high pitch. On the other hand, satiation for primary reinforcers, mild restriction of movement imposed by loosely draped clothing, gentle stroking, and mild and prolonged auditory and visual stimuli lead to a quiescent behavior, internal and external.

REFERENCES

Brackbill, Yvonne. Experimental research with children in the Soviet Union: a report of a visit. *Amer. Psychol.*, 1960, *15*, 226–233.

Bryan, E. S. Variations in the response of infants during first ten days of postnatal life. *Child Develpm.*, 1930, *1*, 56–77.

Crowell, D. H. Unpublished manuscript. Univer. of Hawaii, 1963.

Crowell, D. H., Peterson, J., & Safely, M. A. An apparatus for infant conditioning research. *Child Develpm.*, 1960, *31*, 47–52.

Dennis, W. A description and classification of the responses of the newborn infant. *Psychol. Bull.*, 1934, *31*, 5–22.

Dennis, W. Infant reactions to restraint. *Trans. N.Y. Acad. Sci.*, 1940, *2*, series II, 202–217.

Disher, D. R. The reactions of newborn infants to chemical stimuli administered nasally. Columbus: *Ohio State Univer. Stud.*, 1934, No. 12, 1–52.

Elkonin, D. B. The physiology of higher nervous activity and child psychology. In B. Simon (Ed.), *Psychology in the Soviet Union*, London: Routledge and Kegan Paul, Ltd., 1957.

Engen, T., Lipsitt, L. P., & Kaye, H. Olfactory responses and adaptation in the human neonate. *J. comp. physiol. Psychol.*, 1963, *56*, 73–77.

Fantz, R. Pattern vision in newborn infants. *Science*, 1963, *140*, 296–297.

Gullickson, G. R. Classical defense conditioning in the human neonate. Unpublished master's thesis, Univ. of Hawaii, 1963.

Gullickson, G. R., & Crowell, D. H. Neonatal habituation to electrotactual stimulation. *J. exp. child Psychol.*, 1964, *1*, 388–396.

Haller, M. W. The reactions of infants to changes in the intensity and pitch of pure tone. *J. genet. Psychol.*, 1932, *40*, 162–180.

Irwin, O. C. The distribution of the amount of motility in young infants between two nursing periods. *J. comp. Psychol.*, 1932, *14*, 415–428.

Irwin, O. C., & Weiss, LaBerta. Studies in infant behavior I. *Univ. of Iowa Stud. child Welf.*, 1934, 9, No. 4, 151–161.

Irwin, O. C., & Weiss, LaBerta. The effect of clothing on the general and vocal activity of the newborn. *Univer. Iowa Stud. child Welf.*, 1934, 9, No. 4, 149–162.

Jensen, K. Differential reactions to taste and temperature stimuli in newborn infants. *Genet. Psychol. Mongr.*, 1932, *12*, 361–479.

Jones, M. C. The development of early behavior patterns in young children. *J. genet. Psychol.*, 1926, *33*, 537–585.

Keen, Rachel. The effects of auditory stimuli on sucking behavior in the human neonate. *J. exp. child Psychol.*, 1964, *1*, 348–354.

Lipsitt, L. P. Learning in the first year of life. In L. P. Lipsitt & C. C. Spiker (Eds.), *Advances in child development and behavior.* Vol. I. New York: Academic Press, 1963.

Lipsitt, L. P., & DeLucia, C. An apparatus for the measurement of specific response and general activity of the human neonate. *Amer. J. Psychol.*, 1960, *73*, 630–632.

Lipsitt, L. P., & Kaye, H. Conditioned sucking in the human newborn. *Psychon. Sci.*, 1964, *1*, 29–30.

Lipsitt, L. P., & Levy, N. Electrotactual threshold in the neonate. *Child Develpm.*, 1959, *30*, 547–554.

Lipsitt, L. P. & Marum, K. D. A study of classical conditioning in the human neonate. Paper read at Eastern Psychol. Assoc. Convention, New York, April, 1960.

Marquis, Dorothy P. Can conditioned responses be established in the newborn infant? *J. genet. Psychol.*, 1931, *39*, 479–492.

Meier, G. W., Bunch, M. E., Nolan, C. Y., & Scheidler, C. H. Anoxia, behavioral development, and learning ability: a comparative-experimental approach. *Psychol. Monogr.*, 1960, *74*.

Morgan, S. S., & Morgan, J. J. B. An examination of the development of certain adaptive behavior patterns in infants. *J. Pediat.*, 1944, *25*, 168–177.

Pratt, K. C. The neonate. In L. Carmichael (Ed.), *Manual of child psychology.* (2nd Ed.) New York: Wiley, 1954.

Pratt, K. C., Nelson, Amalie K., & Sun, K. H. *The behavior of the newborn infant.* Columbus: Ohio State Univer. Press, 1930.

Sherman, M., & Sherman, I. C. *The process of human behavior.* New York: Norton, 1929.

Stubbs, Esther M. The effect of the factors of duration, intensity, and pitch of sound stimuli on responses of new-born infants. *Univ. Iowa Stud. child Welf.*, 1934, 9, No. 4.

Watson, J. B. *Psychology: from the standpoint of a behaviorist.* Philadelphia: Lippincott, 1919.

Weiss, LaBerta. Effects of light and sound upon neonatal activity. *Univer. Iowa Stud. child Welf.*, 1934, 9, No. 4, 1–71.

Wickens, D. D., & Wickens, Carol D. A study of conditioning in the neonate. *J. exp. Psychol.*, 1940, 26, 94–102.

Woodworth, R. S., & Schlossberg, H. *Experimental psychology.* (Rev. ed.) New York: Holt, 1954.

4

Further Considerations in the Psychological Analysis of the Neonate

The preceding chapter discussed the ways in which environmental events interact with the neonate, and briefly described his biological structure and physiological functioning. The psychological behavior of the neonate was considered in relation to known variables and to setting conditions of which they are or might prove to be a function. Does the account gloss over some essential psychological characteristics of the neonate? Nothing was said about the neonate's personality, drives, intelligence, state of consciousness, or native morality. Let us consider these possibilities separately.

PERSONALITY

Does the neonate have a personality? Obviously we cannot answer this question without a clear idea of what it is that we are to judge. It is better to ask: "What is the precise meaning of 'personality'?" Unfortunately, a satisfactory answer is difficult to obtain. Allport (1937) says that there are over 50 definitions of the term. In view of the date of his estimate, this is obviously a conservative one. In looking over the multitude of definitions and descriptions, however, one thing seems to be clear. Most definitions treat personality as an internal variable, as something inside the individual which his behavior merely expresses. Thus, it usually is assigned the function of *causing and guiding* behavior and adjustment. For example, McClelland (1951) defines personality as made up of hypothetical perceptions, schemata, and drives. For Allport (1937, p. 8), "Personality is a dynamic organization within the individual of those psychophysical systems that determine his unique adjustments to his environment. . . . Personality *is* something and *does* something. . . . It is what lies *behind* specific acts and *within* the individual." Freud (1949) said that personality is a hypothetical construct consisting of the id, ego, and superego, and might some day be shown to be coordinated with parts of the brain. For Murray (1951), "personality" is a hypothetical structure of the mind which may be "biologically defined as the governing organ, or superordinate institution, of the body. As such it is located in the brain. No brain, no personality" (p. 267).

Defining a psychological term as an intervening variable—hypothetical or otherwise—yields no advantages in a natural science approach. Hence a functional definition of personality is preferred, such as the one by Lundin (1961, p. 8): "Personality is that organization of unique behavioral equipment an individual has acquired under the special conditions of his development."

The newborn has little or no organization of unique behavioral equipment acquired under the special conditions of his development. This conclusion seems reasonable, since the "organization of unique behavioral equipment and the special conditions of his development" refers mostly to social behavior and social conditions. The neonate's psychological history from the time of viability has not yet been demonstrated to be impressive, and certainly it does not include much social interaction even in the case of multiple births.

What is seen at birth and often is mistaken for personality is the infant's unique anatomical and physiological make-up. Although there are striking similiarities among newborns of the same race, each, of course, may be characterized in his own anatomical and physiological terms. Differences of this sort are better referred to as individual biological differences.

Each neonate has, of course, a unique biological make-up. His unique organization of psychological equipment has yet to evolve. It will do so as a consequence of his personal interactional history, which will include the effects of contingencies with schedules of primary and acquired reinforcement, involving punishment, eliciting stimuli, emotional operations, and setting events.

DRIVES

"Drive" is usually referred to in two basic ways: (1) as a *hypothetical variable* which supposedly explains or accounts for behavior (such as a "need" for self-expression, which *might* explain constant talking about one's self), and (2) as a *relationship* between setting events and changes in stimulus-response relationships (such as the elapse of time since the last feeding and increases in motility). We use the term in the second way, as a description of functional relationships. From this point of view the neonate may be said to have drives in the sense that the setting events of deprivation and satiation of food and water, sleep, activity, air, and aversive stimulation are shown (1) to produce changes in overt behavior such as sucking, motility level, and changes in physiological behavior such as respiration and heart rates, and (2) to inhibit or facilitate other interactions, such as paying attention to the movement of a toy or the sound of a music box.

However, let us at least note a few of the more frequently discussed hypothetical drives—self-actualization, orality, and love and affection.

Self-Actualization

Jersild (1960) describes the self-actualization drive in these words: "The organism is endowed with an impulse to mobilize its resources and put them to use. According to this position the child is not just trying to maintain a state of equilibrium—he invites a state of disequilibrium—he seeks to put potential abilities to use, to enter into experiences that employ his capacities for doing, thinking and feeling, and for sharing with others" (p. 13).

The concept of an impulse to mobilize resources and put them to use is impossible to define independently of their supposed cause. The existence of such impulses is usually inferred from observing changes in behavior. Changes in the child "for the better" are equated to better use of the self-actualizing impulse, and changes "for the worse" to inhibition of this drive. But the factors which produce such changes in behavior for "the better or worse" are *environmental* events and these are not mentioned as part of the "self-actualization drive." The child may develop into an erudite, enthusiastic, forceful, and perceptive individual or into an ignorant, lethargic, and insensitive character. The problem is to discover the events which cause such development, not to label the development as well or poorly "mobilized" after it has occurred.

In short, the accounting of psychological development will be better advanced if, in place of arguing that the child grows this way or that way because of the inferred state of his self-actualization drive, research were conducted to demonstrate empirical relationships between specific circumstances and specific behavioral changes.

Orality

Some writers, particularly those who adhere to a psychoanalytic theory of development, claim that the infant is born with an oral drive. Sucking behavior is said to satisfy both nutritional and psychosexual needs.

Freud (1949) wrote:

> The baby's obstinate persistence in sucking gives evidence at an early stage of a need for satisfaction which, although it originates from and is stimulated by the taking of nourishment, nevertheless seeks to obtain pleasure independently of nourishment and for that reason may and should be described as 'sexual' (p. 28).

Thus, if an infant fails to have adequate sucking experiences during feeding, more sucking behavior should take place between feedings; and if the infant is prevented from gratifying his oral needs, he may in later life suffer maladjustment or strike upon an adjustment which would involve a high degree of oral activity, e.g., playing the clarinet or chewing his fingernails.

This concept is dubious for at least two reasons. First, the logic involved is obscure. It states that an event in infancy, inadequate sucking experience, is the determining condition for establishing maladjustment of a certain type of adjustment in later life, as in adolescence or adulthood. The difficulty is not with the proposition that early events influence future events, but with the long time span postulated and the disregard for the possible influences of other events that occur during the period. These features of the formulation, the long interval and the extreme complexity of intervening events, make it practically impossible to conduct an efficiently designed study in which the other, presumably more involved events could be somehow nullified and thereby permit an evaluation of the alleged relationship. Indeed, this type of hypothesis depreciates the role of practically all intervening events except those classified as severe or traumatic.

The second reservation about the concept of oral drive is empirical—the results from the limited research accomplished to date do not support it. For example, a survey by Sears (1943) of the influence of early experiences in general on later adjustments produced negative conclusions. An experimental study of the dependency between amount of sucking to obtain milk and the amount of sucking exhibited between feedings showed no relationship (Davis, Sears, Miller, & Brodbeck, 1948). A group of 60 babies was divided into three sub-groups of 20 each, one being fed by cup, one by bottle, and one by breast during the first ten days of life. Under this plan those fed by cup should have the least amount of sucking experience, those by bottle an intermediate amount, and those by breast the most. It would be expected, on the basis of an oral-drive concept, that sucking at other times should be strongest in the cup-fed group and weakest in the breast-fed group. The results showed no statistically reliable differences between the two groups with respect to amount of spontaneous oral activity. Furthermore, the breast-fed infants developed a stronger rather than a weaker sucking response than the cup-fed and bottle-fed groups. In addition there was no reliable difference between the cup-fed and bottle-fed groups in this respect.

The literature of child development abounds with surveys of other problems of orality: breast feeding versus bottle feeding, early weaning versus late weaning, and routine feeding versus demand feeding. Data on these issues do not provide convincing answers. (For an interesting review of the literature, see Caldwell, 1964.) All that can be said at present is that differences in other day-to-day practices of mothers are probably more important conditions than any of these techniques. For example, it seems unbelievable that early weaning in itself would invariably lead to disastrous effects. It should be far more important to determine whether the infant is being weaned (early or late) on a plan involving differential positive reinforcement of successive approximations to new feeding responses, or on one involving extinction and aversive contingencies.

Love and Affection

The concept of a love drive is closely related to the concept of an oral drive; it stems from the same theory of psychological development. It is claimed that infants require large quantities of love (meaning warmth and affection, not merely caretaking nor, of course, sex); in effect, babies are supposed to have a hunger for love similar to their hunger for food. Too little food implies physical starvation and death; similarly, too little love is said to allow psychological starvation and wasting away. The positive side of the analogy is also pursued: just as a good supply of food promotes robust physical growth, similarly a bountiful supply of love produces expansion of intellect and personality.

We cannot say whether the human infant has a need for affection similar to his need for food. The few studies of children reared with little or no affection (Spitz, 1949) cannot easily be accepted as showing that their often unusual subsequent development can be attributed simply to a lack of love in their earlier lives: selection factors and other important environmental variables have also been involved. There are, for example, studies of infants reared in apparently loveless foundling homes; these infants were reported to have suffered a high death rate or to have shown marked retardation in physical and psychological development. But these infants also suffered a marked lack of stimulation of a great variety of kinds. Furthermore, mysterious epidemics and dietary deficiencies are possible even in the nurseries of the most technically advanced countries of the world; the children in these studies lived (or died) in countries of far less advanced medical competence.[1]

There are other studies of children who, in retrospect, seem to have had little in the way of an affectionate rearing during their infancy. Subsequently, many (not all) of them were described as maladjusted, emotionally unresponsive, devoid of interpersonal relationships, aggressive, psychopathic, unmanageable, and—significantly, we think—attention-seekers (e.g., Goldfarb, 1944).

Attention and affection are established as positive social reinforcers by separate processes. A child who is reinforced by nearness and attention of adults is likely to develop behaviors which succeed in producing these stimuli most efficiently. Bad, undesirable, irritating, shocking, and delinquent behaviors typically succeed in bringing an adult near and in getting his attention. It is a rare institution which will let such behavior go unnoticed. If the attendants are busy (and they usually are, as well as being underpaid and overburdened) they may well let good behavior go by without reaction or with a casual token of approval and appreciation; they may then move off to attend to somebody who is "really" in need, i.e., showing signs of maladjustment, destruction, or otherwise delinquent behavior. Giving attention under these circumstances is not usually followed by behavior that might be described as affectionate. In many instances affection might not be established at all as a social reinforcer. In short, there may exist a program of differential reinforcement for all of the behaviors noted in these studies. And when the investigator observes that while the children seek his attention frequently, but are indifferent to whether there are any approving or demanding components within it, he may conclude that these children are unable to form "emotional" bonds with people.

Thus, we would agree that a child raised without displays of

[1] Despite the points we have noted above, it is not uncommon to find accounts of these children comparing them with a group of infants reared by their own mothers in an institution, and declaring that both groups shared "adequate" or "excellent" conditions of nutrition, hygiene, medical care, and housing, and thus differed only in terms of mother love. The comparison group developed normally in all ways. Spitz's description of the conditions in which the foundling children lived raises questions about such a simple conclusion.

love and affection is likely to become a distinctive child. He is likely to be reinforced by all kinds of attention, not just that specific (and somewhat rarer) form of it called affection, respect, or approval by adults. Such a child would have a poor prognosis for future development since he is likely to develop undesirable rather than desirable behaviors. But it does not imply that the child is necessarily maladjusted or otherwise psychologically deformed. He is simply (and sadly) insensitive to a particular social reinforcer, affection-approval, and he fails to learn those responses which gain approval differentially, and fails to suppress those responses which lose it. He learns, of course, according to the same laws of learning that explain the learned development of all other children; only the details of those laws will be different (i.e., the specific responses involved in the contingencies). He will, in effect, learn exactly what he is taught by those who approach him and attend to him. But he will fail to restrict his behaviors to those which produce respect rather than other forms of attention.

In this context a study by Harriet Rheingold (1956) is of significance. She was interested in studying the effect of mothering infants in an institutional setting. Her subjects were 16 babies at six months of age. Eight were designated as "controls"–i.e., they were handled in the usual way; eight were "experimental," i.e., given special treatment. The investigator herself mothered the eight babies in the experimental group five days a week for eight weeks. She spent about 7½ hours a day changing them, feeding them, playing with them, and putting them to sleep. In fact, she spent more time with them than mothers ordinarily have time for. During the study she was in contact with each baby in the experimental group 23% of the time, whereas the other babies in the control group had contact with the regular institutional personnel about 7% of the time. There was another difference. She was the primary person interacting with the experimental group, while there were many different individuals looking after the "control" babies. After the study was completed, the groups were evaluated in terms of their physical growth and their social responsiveness to the investigator and to other adults. It was found that the babies in the experimental group were more responsive to her than to other individuals. However, the less regular handling of the "control" babies did not cause poor physical growth or depression. These babies were indeed getting along well. The experimental group did show more alertness and reactivity to the investigator. It is clear that positive and non-aversive social relationships with a mother (i.e., affection) can have beneficial social effects. It is just this type of research that is needed to yield more specific information rather than to postulate unsatisfied drives.

INTELLIGENCE

"Intelligence," like "personality" and "drive," is variously defined in the literature of child development. Whether or not the neonate is born with a fixed level of intelligence rests heavily on the type of definition that is accepted. We have no factual reasons to consider intelligence as a thing (e.g., a group of calls). A workable concept of the term would require a thorough description of intellectual behaviors; almost certainly these behaviors would be found to relate to a multitude of psychological interactions, historical and current.

It is relatively easy to make such a description of the behavior of children after they have some postnatal history. It is more difficult to apply it to the neonate since our description will consist of individual variations in simple stimulus-response relationships reviewed in Chapter 3. For example, what light intensity is necessary to arouse a reliable visual response in an infant? How rapidly does the neonate adapt to that level of intensity? What is the level at which he shows stable responding? What is the latency, amplitude, and duration of his responses? Many would wonder if such behaviors deserve the label "intellectual" or "intelligent." However, answers to these questions would yield statements not unlike Piaget's concept of the reflex stage of sensorimotor intelligence (Piaget, 1954).

Perhaps this is all that can be said about the intelligence of a neonate. If so, neonatal intelligence becomes a rather limited concept, and one not easily distinguished from the idea that neonates differ from one another in terms of individual biological characteristics relevant to simple motor responses.

It might be, of course, that measures of simple stimulus-response relationships in the neonate are *indications* of intelligence in that they can be shown to relate to scores on intelligence tests obtained later in development. Research, however, shows that such measures taken on infants (in infant-intelligence tests such as the Gesell & Amatruda [1941] and Cattell [1940] scales) are *not* related to scores on child-intelligence tests such as the Stanford-Binet (Terman & Merrill, 1937, 1960) and the Wechsler (1949) administered to children between three and five years of age and older (Bayley, 1958).

The reason for this is straightforward. Many of the items in an infant-intelligence scale, which may be administered to infants as young as one month of age, are similar to (and indeed derived from) accounts of simple stimulus-response relationships. On the other hand, many of the items on a child-intelligence test, designed for youngsters three years old and above, do not involve simple stimulus-response relationships. Instead, the typical child-intelligence test is designed to resemble school work. It has been known for some time, since about 1904, that achievement in reading, writing, and arithmetic does not correlate to any significant degree with simple stimulus-response relationships (such as sensitivity and reaction time to auditory and visual stimuli).

Some view with surprise this lack of correspondence between intelligence measures taken in infancy and in early childhood. Disappointment is engendered only in those who assume that intelligence tests measure something more than behavior, i.e., something "behind" behavior "inside" the organism that causes intelligent behavior, and that this "something" is fixed within the individual and therefore should be detected by many measures of behavior. (After all, the titles on all of these tests include the same word, "intelligence.") Psychological scales—intelligence, aptitude, and others—measure relationships between complex stimuli and responses, and statements summarizing the results of such relationships have practical value only to the extent that they correlate with performances in practical activities, such as school work or vocational training.

Some may wish to argue that intelligence should be defined simply as the speed of learning. This may be a reasonably good definition for certain purposes, but it is not serviceable for determining whether the neonate has intelligence. Evaluation of speed of learning in the newborn at present would be limited to respondent conditioning (which is at best unstable) and to the slim possibility of the beginnings of operant conditioning. It would therefore not be practical, at present, to try to classify neonates on the basis of their speed of learning. More important than such practical considerations are some factual ones concerning the speed of learning. In general, learning goes faster when strong reinforcers are used under moderate deprivation, when appropriate schedules are imposed, when the discriminative stimuli involved are clear and consistent, and when the learner already has learned some of the basic components of similar problems. Testable infants may differ in all these ways; hence their speed of learning will differ for these reasons. Do they therefore differ in intelligence? In particular, if two comparable infants are learning that to lift the right arm will produce milk, and one is deprived of milk for two hours and the other for four hours is the latter therefore more intelligent? He will probably learn faster.

CONSCIOUSNESS

Is the neonate *conscious* of what is going on around him? Is he *aware* of the happenings about him? It is difficult to say.

Our answer must depend on the meaning of the term defined so as to be consistent with a functional analysis.[2] In general the terms "conscious" and "aware" refer to something that an individual describes (usually in verbal terms) which is private to him, and to him alone. What is communicated to others is some statement about what the person is doing, plans to do, has done, feels, or has felt. Usually when a person talks along these lines, we say that he is conscious or aware of himself.

Since the newborn does not have the equipment to engage in

[2] Like emotion, personality, drive, and intelligence, the concept of consciousness comes from the everyday language practices of a culture which generally accepts *as fact* that mental events take place in the body and cause behavior. This assumption is often stated this way: behavior is not important; it is merely symptomatic of important psychic events occurring inside the individual. This is not, of course, the viewpoint of scientific psychology, nor of this book.

verbal behavior, we cannot conclude that he is capable of conscious behavior. We may infer from this other behavior that he does not feel comfortable in the presence of strangers, or is in a state of confusion, or sees the world as a blurred mass, but in doing so we are merely describing his behavior, and have no reason to suppose that he is in any sense aware of (discriminating) his own behavior. To do so would merely be indulging in what might be called "adultomorphic" thinking—attributing adult reactions and traits to the infant. More important, we are indulging in untestable speculation that can lead to naught.

To say that the newborn does not have consciousness does not deny the universally accepted assumption that early interactions (history) play a part in affecting present behavior. The interactional history of an individual always plays a part in determining his present reactions. This is true whether the individual can or cannot react verbally to his own behavior.

If one wishes to view early unverbalized reactions as a significant part of *the unconscious,* and claim that later behavior is in part determined by it, his thinking would be consistent with psychoanalytic theory. Aside from the fact that such a stand makes a "thing" out of interaction sequences and attaches still another label (but no new information) to stimulus-behavior relationships, it is not inconsistent with a functional analysis of behavior.

The following words from Munn (1955) serve as an appropriate summary:

> The student of behavior does not, of course, deny that consciousness exists. It may exist even in the amoeba. He claims, however, that since it is beyond direct observation, and inferences regarding it cannot be checked, consciousness must remain outside the sphere of scientific psychology (p. 7).

INNATE MORALITY

Some writers, such as Rousseau and Montaigne, have claimed that infants have a native tendency to be good, God-fearing, social, free, relaxed, and normal. Others have maintained that they are born bad and sinful (St. Augustine), or antisocial (Lambroso).

Infants do not "come into the world" with tendencies to be

either good or bad, but instead arrive in a completel with respect to innate morality. Note that terms such "bad" are labels attached to a wide class of behaviors. stitutes a class is determined by the practices of the c it is likely that an individual is labeled good insofar a forces other members of the group and bad insofar as h sive (Skinner, 1953). Thus the usual sequence of events le a judgment on morality is somewhat as follows: Many things the child does with respect to people and prope described as "good" or "bad" by parents, teachers, and othe look after him. Later these people sum up and say he is a go a bad child; then they claim that the specific good or bad beh *results* from that summary "fact." Of course, to name a clas behavior is not the same as explaining its causation.

It is easy to justify beliefs about good and bad behavior on t basis that the child was "born that way." The alternate view th these behaviors are dependent on the child's history, the curren situation, and the practices of the group (actually, the "practices of the group" are a part of the child's history and current situation) requires a reexamination of our thinking.

Thus, the newborn does not have a natural tendency to be good or bad. But he is born into a culture which does have a strong (but acquired) tendency to judge him and then let the judgment *explain* his behavior as well.

SUMMARY

Summing up what has been presented in this and the previous chapter, the neonate is viewed as a biological organism with special and individual anatomical and physiological characteristics which are shaped by the interactions of heredity (genotype) and organic-physical conditions and events starting at the moment of fertilization. Neonatal interactions consist of a unified stimulus-response system and environmental events. Some of these interactions are essentially biological or neurological; that is, they are, for the most part, specific responses to specific stimulations applied to the body. Such interactions are not conditionable. Other physiological reactions are potentially conditionable (i.e., shown o be conditionable in later development) along the lines of respondent and operant principles. They include general reactions (e.g., "excitement" behavior to sudden and intensive stimuli), segmental reactions (e.g., foot withdrawal in response to electrotactile stimulation) and smooth-muscle changes (e.g., increase in respiratory rate in response to sudden and strong stimulation).

Visual, auditory, olfactory, gustatory, and tactual stimuli elicit reliably recordable responses, although adaptation is relatively rapid. It is still a question whether the respondent and operant behavior of the neonate can be conditioned and maintained in a stable fashion.

Satiation and deprivation of homeostatic reinforcers such as food, water, air, activity, and sleep, systematically affect the neonate's behavior. Also, a variety of emotional operations can produce, on one hand, a complex reaction described as the activation syndrome and "excitement" behavior; and on the other, a pattern of internal and external responses generally designated as quiescence.

Aside from his individual biological characteristics the neonate cannot be said to have a personality, a fixed amount of innate intelligence, innate psychic drives, consciousness, or an innate morality.

From birth on, psychological development comes about as the consequence of the maturing biological individual (changes in anatomical structure and physical functioning, which are given the status of participating independent variables and setting events), physical and social conditions, past and present. Biological and psychological interactions take place at the same time and function with respect to each other in an interdependent fashion.

The social aspects of the neonate's future experiences are particularly influential. They

1. Control the primary reinforcers and set the conditions under which acquired reinforcers will be developed.
2. Establish and maintain emotionalizing operations and contingencies.
3. Shape behavior (manner, customs, verbal and motor skills, achievements, attitudes, etc.) that will be acceptable to the group.
4. Set the occasions upon which prescribed forms of behavior will be reinforced or punished.

If desired, these interactions may be conceptualized as personality, intelligence level, "high-order" drives, consciousness, and morality.

REFERENCES

Allport, G. W. *Personality*. New York: Holt, 1937.

Bayley, Nancy. Value and limitation of infant testing. *Children,* 1958, *5,* 129–133.

Caldwell, Bettye M. The effects of infant care. In M. L. Hoffman & Lois W. Hoffman (Eds.), *Review of child development research*. New York: Russell Sage Foundation, 1964.

Cattell, Psyche. *The measurement of intelligence of infants and young children*. New York: Psychol. Corp., 1940.

Davis, H. V., Sears, R. R., Miller, H. C., & Brodbeck, A. J. Effects of cup, bottle, and breast feeding upon newborn infants. *Pediatrics,* 1948, *3,* 549–558.

Freud, S. *Outline of psychoanalysis*. New York: Norton, 1949.

Gesell, A., & Amatruda, G. S. *Developmental diagnosis*. New York: Hoeber, 1941.

Goldfarb, W. The effects of early institutional care on adolescent personality. *Amer. J. Orthopsychiat.*, 1944, *14,* 441–447.

Jersild, A. T. *Child psychology*. (5th ed.) New York: Prentice-Hall, 1960.

Lundin, R. W. *Personality*. New York: Macmillan, 1961.

McClelland, D. C. *Personality*. New York: Sloane Associates, 1951.

Munn, N. L. *The evolution and growth of human behavior*. Boston: Houghton Mifflin, 1955.

Murray, H. A. Some basic psychological assumptions and conceptions. *Dialectica,* 1951, *5,* 266–292.

Piaget, J. *The construction of reality in the child*. New York: Basic Books, 1954.

Rheingold, Harriet L. The modification of social responsiveness in institutional babies. *Monogr. Soc. Res. Child Developm.*, 1956, *21,* No. 2 (Whole No. 63).

Sears, R. R. Survey of objective studies of psychoanalytic concepts. *Soc. Sci. Res. Council Bull.*, 1943, No. 51.

Skinner, B. F. *Science and human behavior*. New York: Macmillan, 1953.

Spitz, R. A. The role of ecological factors in emotional development in infancy. *Child Develpm.*, 1949, *20,* 145–156.

Terman, L. M., & Merrill, Maud A. *Measuring intelligence: a guide to the administration of the new revised Stanford-Binet tests of intelligence.* Boston: Houghton Mifflin, 1937.

Terman, L. M., & Merrill, Maud A. *Stanford-Binet intelligence scale: manual for the third revision, Form L-M.* Boston: Houghton Mifflin, 1960.

Wechsler, D. *The Wechsler intelligence scale for children.* New York: Psychol. Corp., 1949.

5

Processes of Behavioral Elaboration

In Chapter 3 we characterized the neonate as a possessor of a considerable catalogue of behaviors. We could say little about the stimuli controlling them. It is clear, however, that the behavior of the neonate, which is simple, limited, and in many respects different from that of other organisms, develops into complex, extended, and largely individualistic behavior which characterizes the adult. How does this come about?

One answer: the behaviors of the infant are modified to become the behaviors of the adult. Another answer: new behaviors emerge. Both of these answers hold traditional places in the history of speculation about child development. The purpose of this chapter is to examine and review some of the mechanisms which either shape pre-existing behavior into different and more complex forms, or account for the emergence of entirely new patterns of response. In either event, the emphasis is on the *elaboration* of behavior. Development consists of transitions from simple and few behaviors, responsive to correspondingly simple and few stimuli, to complex and many response chains intricately related to vast arrays of controlling stimuli. Hence, each behavioral process examined is viewed not merely as a mechanism of behavior change, but also as a means for producing increasingly elaborate behavior.

The discussion is limited to three mechanisms of behavior modification: (1) heredity, (2) organism-environmental interactions involving respondent conditioning, and (3) organism-environmental interactions involving operant conditioning.

HEREDITARY PROCESSES

One of the oldest ideas about child development is that human characteristics and behavior are inherited through the individual's line of ancestry. It is ordinarily not questioned that the human body form (one head, two arms and legs, five fingers per hand, five toes per foot, etc.) is an invariant inheritance of the species; that sex, blood characteristics, hair and eye color are more variable inheritances characterizing large sub-groups of the species; and that many traits are highly individualized inheritances of specific members of the species. Nor is it doubted that many inherited characteristics do not appear in the infant, but emerge at a later stage of development, through an unfolding process termed maturation.

Such phenomena have been demonstrated repeatedly in experimental breeding programs with animals, for practical, scientific, and esthetic reasons. Man has bred cows for milk or meat; horses for pulling power or speed; dogs for herding, retrieving, or appearance; and fruitflies for long or short wings and answers to genetic riddles. Consequently, it has been reasonable to look for patterns of anatomical structure, biological function, and behavior to appear in man throughout his development from infancy to adulthood, independently of much of his experience with the environment.

But it is at the same time apparent that man's behavior is also modified by experiences. Consequently, a classic question arose early in the study of child behavior and development, and has literally plagued the field ever since: Which specific behaviors of a man are determined by his ancestry, and how much? Some students of child development have answered the question, unhesitatingly, with replies ranging from "All behaviors, to any degree" to "Few behaviors, and not much." Others have offered less extreme replies, but rephrased the question in a manner which seems to divide behaviors into an unspecified fraction which is solely the product of ancestry, and the rest which is solely the result of environmental action. This partition of the disputed territory of behavior never satisfied either claimant, however, and border wars have been common. Naturally, peacemakers have appeared who attempted to give all behaviors to both sides, suggesting that equally great modifications of any behavior could be accomplished by both breeding and experience, or both "nature and nurture."

Our account thus far has noted that during prenatal development a great deal of interaction might be expected between biological and physiological events originating in the fetus's genes. However, we could not state the details of such interactions, and could only point to their high probability and the difficult technical problems involved in studying them. This, in effect, is a theme which could be restated at the outset of every new topic dealt with here, *for the possibility of genetic interaction with other variables never ceases to be a likely characteristic of development.*

We have not attempted to develop that possibility, however, since the technical problems involved in effective investigations of the appropriate sort seem insurmountable. It may be concluded that the problems of inheritance, maturation, and instinct are not adequately treated by students of human development because at the present they have no effective technique for dealing with them.

Evidence for the role of ancestry in the behavioral development of organisms other than man can be gathered by selectively breeding successive generations, solely with a view toward intensifying or diminishing the appearance of a given behavior. Results from studies employing this method show that the characteristic behavior of a particular offspring may be a function of the appearance or non-appearance of that behavior in his ancestry, and that ancestry may be deliberately arranged by the experimenter to analyze such relationships. With respect to human development, there is no possibility of systematically mating selected individuals over a dozen or more generations simply to see if the characteristics of their offspring can be determined thereby. Hence, if the role of heredity in determining psychological behavior is to be studied, other methods must be used. Unfortunately, the other methods, as will be seen, are not powerful. They do not give unambiguous answers about the role of ancestry in the development of human psychological behavior.

The most notable of alternative methods are those which involve identical and fraternal twins in various interactions with their environments. Twins are used because they permit some degree of knowledge about genetic variables. Identical twins result from the division of a single fertilized egg; therefore, they have identical genetic composition. Fraternal twins result from the fertilization of two eggs by two sperms, and thus represent two random samples from the genetic pools of the parents. Three types of studies have evolved from the possible ways in which the development of the two kinds of twins may be related to environmental events.

The Reared-Apart Twins Method

The first method takes advantage of the unfortunate circumstance that some twins are raised, most of their lives, by different foster parents. Some students of child development have seen this unusual circumstance in the developmental history of children as a ready-made experimental design to untangle the relative roles of heredity and environment in child behavior.

The logic inherent in these studies moves along these general lines: Identical twins have identical genes, and therefore any behaviors caused primarily by heredity must be extremely similar in both of these twins, despite their different environment. Behaviors influenced primarily by experience, by contrast, are likely to be quite different in these twins, since they have been reared by different foster parents in different places. Since this is a matter of relative difference, a statistical approach is necessary: Many pairs of identical twins reared apart must be observed, so that behaviors due mainly to environmental processes will have a chance (within the group of twins) to develop differently, at least in those twins whose respective foster parents treat them differently in the ways which matter from a developmental point of view.

For comparison, some investigators have used fraternal twins reared by their natural parents within the same home. Thus one comparison could compare the differences between identical twins reared apart to differences between fraternal twins reared together. On one hand, if a behavior is primarily due to heredity, it would seem that identical twins should be similar, despite their environmental differences, while fraternal twins, who can have different genes, should, on the average, differ, despite the common effect of similar environments. On the other hand, if a behavior is primarily due to environment, then the identical or fraternal characteristic of the twins becomes irrelevant. The fact that the fraternals have been reared together should show them to be more similar than the identicals reared apart. Thus, it is said, a simple test for the influence of heredity on behavior is available: when identical twins reared apart are more similar in some behavior than fraternals reared together, the behavior is due to heredity; when fraternals reared together are more similar than identicals reared apart, the behavior is due to environment.

On the basis of this line of reasoning, intelligence has been said to be primarily a product of heredity, since identical twins reared apart have shown more similarity in IQ scores than fraternal twins reared together (Newman, Freeman, & Holzinger, 1937). This conclusion is no more compelling than the assurance that the environments of the identical twins were more dissimilar than the environments of the fraternal twins. On the face of it, children reared together would seem to have a better chance of sharing many common experiences than children reared in different families. However, this "global approach" to the actions of environmental events falls short of the requirements for adequate psychological analysis. *It does not analyze what specific actions of the environment might affect the specific behavior involved in the development of intelligence.* Such specificity would be required to determine that the experiences were indeed more similar for the fraternal twins reared together than for the identical twins reared apart.

For example, suppose that early disruption of social relationships could have a marked effect on the later intellectual development of a child. Then identical twins reared apart would have such experiences *in common,* because they would have lost their parents at an early age and would probably have lived in an institution for some time, awaiting assignment to the "different" environments of their respective foster parents. In this sense, they have similar early environments. The question then requires an answer to another question: What is the effect, if any, of early experiences on intelligence? We cannot answer this question. An answer is needed, however, and to secure it the investigator will have to study the effects of early environment on the developing intellectual behavior of babies, rather than the effects of genetic variables.

The Twin-Family Method

A second variety of twin study, the twin-family method, involves not only twins, but other members of the family. The question in these studies becomes, do persons of closer family (genetic) connection show greater similarity in the behavior than persons of more distant connection? If a behavior is largely the product of inheritance, then identical twins should be extremely similar in displaying such behavior; fraternal twins and ordinary siblings should be much less so, half-siblings still less so, and so on. In other words, a close correlation between genetic similarity and behavioral similarity is said to show the causal role of genetic variables in the determination of the behavior. This line of thinking has been used to suggest that schizophrenic behavior is more clearly related to ancestry than to experience (Kallman, 1946).

The claim that schizophrenic disorders have a genetic origin rests heavily on the assumption that there are no effective systematic environmental influences involved. But it is not unreasonable to take the position that the closer the genetic relationship of two individuals, the more likely that their environments would be similar. Thus it is suggested that identical twins (being alike in sex and many aspects of physical appearance) would in all likelihood be treated similarly by their social environment; whereas, fraternal twins (alike in age but frequently differing in sex and various other physical characteristics) would be treated differently by others.

The soundness of this line of thinking requires study of the relative similarities and differences of specific environmental-organism interactions of identical and fraternal twins and of other relatives. The interactions should be studied with particular reference to those environmental factors hypothesized to cause schizophrenic behavior. The student of the genetic determiners of behavior is again asked to turn to an investigation of the possible effects of environmental actions.

The Co-Twin Method

The third type of twin study, the co-twin design, involves a procedure in which a pair of identical twins is selected and one is arbitrarily treated as the "experimental" twin, the other as the "control." The experimental twin is given special training in the acquisition of some behavior neither twin has previously learned. The objective of this approach is to provide a specially arranged environment that would produce the behavior, if it can be produced at all through experience alone. The control twin receives no such extra training experience, so that time alone is given opportunity to produce the behavior in question. If precocious practice succeeds in producing the behavior in the experimental twin, that behavior is sensitive to environmental action. If it fails, it may be thought that the behavior in question cannot be merely taught, and requires time to elapse so that maturational processes can have effects. It might then be said that the behavior is highly dependent on genetic factors.

The co-twin method can also show that certain behaviors are susceptible to experience, if the results show that the experimental twin develops the response in question at a faster rate than the control twin. However, when the twins show similar rates of development and at the same time, nothing much may be concluded. Such a no-difference finding may be due to the fact that the behavior is not yet amenable to experience; or it may be that the method of instruction employed by the experimenters was not appropriate or adequately programmed. Despite this second possibility, practically all studies resulting in a failure to find a difference between the twins of a co-twin study have led the investigators to conclude that the behavior under study is sensitive primarily to inheritance and only secondarily to experience (e.g., Gesell & Thompson, 1929; McGraw, 1935).

The literature of developmental psychology and education contains numerous studies in which straightforward methods of instruction fail in a given child, while another approach succeeds.

Most teachers have learned a number of paths toward the successful teaching of a new skill to young children and an even greater number of unsuccessful ones. Programmed instruction, as a teaching device, relies heavily on the concept that almost any pattern of behavior can be taught if a proper groundwork is laid down first, and an artful sequence of ideas and examples is used to lead from ignorance to competence. It would seem, then, that any failure in the course of a co-twin study should stimulate attempts with other approaches to instruction or training.

Thus, the conclusion here is the same as that reached in the two previous discussions: The investigator whose interest lies in the possibility of genetic causation of behavior might attempt studies of early environmental-organism interactions involving specific and concrete instances.

Genetic variables cannot be manipulated directly in child research. Direct manipulation would require experimental breeding programs, a technique basic to the science of genetics, but readily available only for laboratory animals. The possibility of experimental breeding of humans is clearly an academic one. The cheerfully haphazard style of our mating practices, while disastrous to the possibilities of drawing conclusions about the genetics of behavior, still seems likely to remain a treasured aspect of our culture.

The twins studies do not involve a direct manipulation of genes, or even a positive definition of the genetic determination of behavior. Instead, such investigations define genetically caused behavior as that behavior which is *un*learned. Twins are studied not because their genes can be manipulated, but because their genes are constant. Environmental variables are changed, or are presumed to have changed, and a lack of ensuing behavioral difference is taken as evidence that the environmental variables may be ignored in favor of genetic variables. Since genetically caused behavior has been defined as "unlearned" behavior in this line of thinking, it is necessary to show that the behavior in question was indeed unlearned, i.e., that *no* manipulation of environmental events produced the behavior.

To show that a bit of behavior was unlearned is practically an infinite task, implying the use of all known techniques of training and the constant invention of new techniques. Thus, an equating of inherited or maturational behavior to unlearned behavior creates the need for studies of environmental-organism interactions, not of the genetic determiners of child behavior and development.

In effect, then, we have largely set aside the role of genetic causation in child development because the experimental techniques available to students of the problem are suitable only to uncover the effects of environmental variables. A more complete science of behavioral development seems possible only with infrahuman subjects.

ENVIRONMENTAL-ORGANISM INTERACTIONS

Respondent Processes

It will be recalled that respondents are strengthened and weakened by certain classes of antecedent stimuli (Vol. I, pp. 27–29). A brief review of the procedure involved is as follows: suppose that some stimulus, S_1, reliably elicits the respondent, R_1. We select another stimulus, S_2, from a large class of stimuli (stimuli that the infant reacts to in a mild fashion), and arrange to have it precede S_1 consistently when S_1 is reacted to by the child. If S_2 comes to elicit the respondent R_1 by itself, unaccompanied by S_1, then respondent conditioning is said to have taken place. The interactional *elaboration* or extension has been accomplished. The baby who shows R_1 to S_1 (which practically all youngsters do) also shows R_1 to S_2, which may be a unique stimulus-response relationship among babies.

For example, we might repeatedly pair the sound of a door-chime with electrotactual stimulation to the foot of an infant. The result would be an infant who kicks his leg whenever visitors come to the door and sound the chime. This infant shows response elaboration in that a kick takes place in relation to one more stimulus (and an unusual one). Most babies kick when electrotactually stimulated on the foot; few kick when they hear a door-chime. In seeing a baby kick to a door-chime, an enthusiastic observer might claim that the baby is excited when visitors come, and hence has a "personality." He is said to be gregarious.

Respondent processes, however, play a limited role in a systematic elaboration of infant behavior. The reasons for this are at least fivefold.

1. In respondent conditioning no new combination of responses is added to the baby's repertory, but only a new functional stimulus. The response to the conditioned eliciting stimulus, S_2, has a somewhat different topography than the response to S_1, the unconditioned eliciting stimulus. Usually the difference is that the conditioned stimulus elicits a weaker or more minimal version of the respondent. The kick following the chime may be smaller than the one followed by application of electrotactual stimulation; or the cry elicited by the electrotactual stimulation may be replaced by only a whimper in response to a conditioned stimulus. Apart from these differences in response characteristics, development on the basis of respondent conditioning is restricted to enlarging the class of stimulus functions.

2. Another limitation of respondent conditioning as a means of interactional elaboration is reflected in the use of words like "if," "usually," "typically," and "possibly" in the preceding description of conditioning procedures. Laboratory investigations of respondent conditioning have pointed consistently to some respondents as unconditionable. That is, none of the extensive and stubborn attempts to produce conditioning of certain respondents (such as the patellar or "knee-jerk" reflex) have succeeded. This has led to the suspicion that currently understood procedures of respondent conditioning simply do not apply to such responses (even though the responses would seem to qualify as respondents on all other grounds). Some respondents may prove to constitute a class in which no development is to be seen, the complete description of these responses being the same in both infant and adult.

3. A third limitation of respondent conditioning as a process in infant development is the fragile nature of such conditioning, as observed in laboratory studies. Following even prolonged conditioning procedures, if the conditioned stimulus is used alone repeatedly to elicit the respondent, it will soon lose its eliciting function through respondent extinction.

There have been certain examples in the clinical literature of psychology which have been tempting to analyze as examples of respondent conditioning, especially those referred to as "psychosomatic" reactions. In these cases the response (wheezing, sneezing, vomiting, etc.) appears to be durably attached to what is thought to be a conditioned stimulus (a mother-in-law, test situation, etc.). If these are in fact instances of respondent conditioning, they contain some factors not yet identified in experimental investigations.

The best that can be said, at present, is that so far as is known, respondent conditioning is a process for enlarging the class of functional stimuli interacting with child behavior only in those situations in which the conditioned stimulus is occasionally and sufficiently reassociated with the already effective antecedent stimulus. Hence, if we expect our baby with a unique history to continue kicking whenever the door-chimes are sounded, we had better continue occasional pairings of the chime with mild electrotactual stimulation to the foot.

4. Another limitation lies in the difficulty of using a conditioned stimulus to establish still more conditioned stimuli (a process usually referred to as higher-order conditioning). To use the previous example: suppose that we have an infant who kicks when the door-chimes are sounded. We might be interested in further elaborating this response, so that he will kick when the dog barks. In principle, the method would be to have dog-barks precede the door-chimes (which elicit the kick). In time, the dog-bark alone should also elicit the kick. In practice, however, such an attempt at conditioning will prove unreliable and brief in duration—if, indeed, it takes place at all. Laboratory experience with higher-order conditioning consistently points to higher-order conditioning as a fragile phenomenon. Thus, its possibilities as a useful mechanism of complex behavioral elaboration seem restricted.

5. A final limitation of respondent conditioning is the fact that the procedures involved apply only to conditionable respondent behaviors. A great deal of the development which must be described is motor, verbal, intellectual, and social; the behaviors involved in these repertories are essentially operant in nature, and are not adequately describable in terms of respondent formulae.

However, respondent conditioning is not wholly unimportant; two comments should be made on its highly essential roles in the interactional processes of development. (1) Operant and respondent behaviors typically occur in continuously intertwined ongoing chains, which may interact with one another in a tight fashion (Vol. I, Ch. 6). Thus the analysis of respondent processes is incomplete without an account of operant processes. (2) The class of respondents usually called "emotional behavior" is so termed primarily because of the nature of the stimuli which elicit them. Red cheeks in a warm room is not an emotional response, but red cheeks in an "embarrassing" situation is. Usually, emotional stimulation consists of the presentation or removal of positive or negative reinforcers. Hence, any condition which adds to the class of reinforcing stimuli is likely to add similarly to the class of emotional stimuli. An account of such interactions constitutes a kind of emotional development; however, the enlargement of the class of reinforcing stimuli is best treated in a discussion of operant rather than respondent behavior. Therefore, we put aside this significant segment of respondent development until Chapter 10, in which we discuss the initial formation of repertories of emotional behavior.

Operant Processes

In both respondent and operant conditioning, the response must exist prior to its elaboration (which is accomplished through stimulus pairing in respondents, and through contingent stimulus consequences in operants). Hence, in both cases, no "new" behaviors are created. Operants may be *chained* to form new "acts," and *shaped* to give new variants, but in both cases the operant existed prior to conditioning. However, new chains of already existing operants are more readily produced than new chains of respondents, and the variety of responses that go into an operant chain is greater than for respondent chains.

It is difficult to make a catalogue of operant behaviors in the newborn. A list of behaviors, largely respondent, has been cited (see Chart 3-1, Chapter 3, page 33). In that list are a few notations of "random" or undifferentiated movements of the whole body or parts of the body. Probably these terms are as close as can be offered at present to a specification of the operant behavior of the neonate. As indicated in the introductory chapter, operant behaviors take on a form primarily because of the shaping influences of appropriate reinforcement contingencies, but respondent behaviors generally have a fairly recognizable shape or topography, even in the neonatal period. The neonate, having undergone few if any reinforcement contingencies, has operants which remain to be shaped by future experiences. Hence the labels applied to the well-formed operants in an older child have little or no application to the aimless, gross, and amorphous responses of the neonate. We note, however, that virtually all of the muscle systems of the newborn display some activity, and no new muscle fibers are formed in later life. We might add that while no new muscle fibers are added (except for the uterus, during pregnancy), the striped muscles of the young infant are small and fragile, and insecurely attached to the bones. Nutrition and interaction add greatly to their size, strength, and durability, resulting in a 38-fold increase in size by adulthood (Arey, 1954).

It follows that the potential for virtually every behavior observed in the adult is present in the newborn. What is required is the *differentiation* (shaping) of these responses into their nearly infinite varieties, the *discrimination* of these differentiated operants to stimuli, thus creating discriminated operants and the *chaining* of these differentiated, discriminated operants into ever longer and more complex chains of greater and greater number and variety.

The processes of differentiation, discrimination, and chaining have been shown to be dependable and readily established and maintained. They do not have the limitations noted with respect to respondent conditioning. Operant conditioning is involved in a vast change in the form and complexity of the infant's responses which may be described as the stringing together of a collection of operants into a chain. An infant may be capable of a variety of arm motions. These may be linked together in slightly different orders to produce behavior described as a wave, a pat, making patty-cake, beating a drum, grabbing a cookie, fending off, sweeping away, etc. The chaining process may be made reliable and durable, and for this reason becomes one of the most ubiquitous processes in behavior.

Furthermore, response strengthening through reinforcement

contingencies produces a durable change. Often an operant lasts for more responses during extinction than it took to build its strength; and with a skillful use of reinforcement schedules, operants may be effectively buttressed against subsequent extinction. In addition, the use of acquired reinforcers to establish new operant chains is straightforward and dependable, as long as the acquired reinforcer maintains its discriminative status for some primary or homeostatic reinforcer (Vol. I, pp. 53–58). And finally, the number of responses controllable by reinforcement contingencies is great indeed.

There is still another reason for emphasizing the role of operant processes in early development. The tremendous wealth of stimulus consequences of behavior which act to influence operants seems to be nowhere as evident as in the young infant. We have referred to the behaviors which are reinforced by this extended range of stimuli as ecological behavior (see Chapter 1). It may be remembered that ecological behavior is behavior controlled by the characteristics of the things with which it interacts, those characteristics usually being inherent in the nature of the things themselves. For example, an infant picks up a block and smacks it sharply down against the floor repeatedly. The inevitable outcomes are sharp noises. These consequences apparently control and momentarily strengthen the responses which produce them. If a layer of padding is slipped under the block to eliminate the sound, the response class is likely to extinguish in short order. A child held in the arms of his father rubs his palm gently over his father's face against the direction of whisker growth. The tactual stimulation produced on the child's palm acts to maintain the behavior briefly. Or the child grabs the parent's nose since this act usually produces a backward jerk of the head. A reach for a parent's glasses typically results in a similar outcome. (The possibility that the head jerk might be the controlling stimulus could be tested by not responding on these occasions, if this is possible.)

Similarly, a young infant squeezes a rubber toy simply because it resists, or because it makes a noise; he shakes a rattle for the same reason. He extracts paper tissues one after another from the container because another always pops out to replace the one pulled. He rubs crayons across paper (and walls) because doing so leaves a mark. He splashes water, bounces balls, and flexes his vocal cords for the consequences they produce.

The point of these examples is both the frequency with which these interactions can be observed in early development and the role of these simple stimulus outcomes in contributing to the strengthening of a wide variety of responses. Operant processes are not restricted to the few interactions an infant's behavior enters into with food, water, and aversive stimuli. Instead, most of the things in his environment, simply because they produce a stimulus feedback when they are responded to, have effects on those responses. This is an operant formula, and one of the most frequently operative of all developmental processes in the minute-to-minute experiences of infants, babies, and young children.

Thus, the procedures of operant conditioning seem to be a promising approach for analyzing the elaboration of behavior. The essential processes are differentiation, discrimination, and chaining; but all of these depend upon reinforcement contingencies. Thus, the first step in our analysis is to survey the stimuli which function as reinforcers for infants in the Universal stage of develment. That is the topic of the next chapter.

REFERENCES

Arey, L. B. *Developmental Anatomy.* (6th ed.) Philadelphia: Saunders, 1954.

Gesell, A., & Thompson, Helen. Learning and growth in identical twins: an experimental study by the method of co-twin control. *Genet. Psychol. Monogr.,* 1929, *6,* 1–124.

Kallman, F. J. The genetic theory of schizophrenia. *Amer. J. Psychiat.,* 1946, *101,* 309–322.

McGraw, Myrtle B. *Growth: a study of Johnny and Jimmy.* New York: Appleton-Century, 1935.

Newman, H. H., Freeman, R. N., & Holzinger, K. J. *Twins: a study of heredity and environment.* Chicago Press, 1937.

6

A Search for Early Reinforcers in the Universal Stage

In principle there is a straightforward procedure for finding out which specific stimuli have reinforcing functions for a given infant. A stimulus is suggested as a candidate; some operant response of the infant to the stimulus is selected as convenient for study. The frequency of occurrence of this response is observed in a given setting until a stable estimate of strength is obtained. Then the stimulus is presented contingent upon every occurrence of this response, and the consequent change in strength of the response is noted.

There are three possible outcomes:

1. There is no change. The stimulus has no reinforcing function (at least, not under the conditions prevailing at the time). It is *neutral.*
2. The response increases in frequency (and decreases when the contingency is stopped). Consistent results of this type show that the stimulus is a *positive reinforcer.*
3. The response decreases in frequency (and increases when the contingency is stopped). The procedure is then reversed: the stimulus is presented and allowed to continue until the response occurs; that is, the response now removes or terminates the stimulus. If, under repetitions of this procedure, the response increases in frequency (and decreases again if the contingency is stopped and the stimulus remains, independent of the response), then the stimulus is a *negative reinforcer.*

These procedures in themselves are clear and easy to follow; however, when the organism under study is the human infant, two serious difficulties arise. The first pertains to the necessity of having some readily observable operant which has a reasonably stable rate of occurrence over time, in order to test the reinforcing function of a stimulus. In Chapter 3 the neonate was characterized as an organism whose operant behavior has yet to be formed (and through reinforcement contingencies, at that). Thus, we need to know what class of responses will serve as an operant in order to discover what class of stimuli will serve as a reinforcer, but first we need to know what reinforcers will strengthen and shape the operant.

This difficulty is a real one. However, findings from current research are helping to overcome it, and future research promises further assistance. One approach is suggested: use one of the few responses of the neonate which has an easily observable topography, such as his sucking response and see if it displays operant characteristics. We have already seen at least one study which suggests that this is a practical procedure, and we shall reconsider it in detail below.

Another approach seems feasible. Create an operant from the "random" movements of the infant's arms, legs, head, or eyes. If we succeed, then the response *was* an operant, and the stimulus employed is established as a reinforcer; if we fail, the outcome is ambiguous.

Still another alternative is to select a response which is gross and vague in its topography (and therefore difficult to observe as a stable response), and attempt to achieve such large effects with stimulus contingencies that the results will be obvious, despite the initial handicaps. Again, success is informative but failure is not. Smiling and vocalizing are two examples of such behavior. Studies involving these responses will also be discussed below.

The second class of difficulties inherent in the problem of specifying the stimuli which will function as reinforcers for the newborn has to do with the fact that some reinforcement contingencies have serious biological implications. For example, it may be suspected that the opportunity to breathe would be a stimulus event with a definite positive reinforcing function. A demonstration of this at the infrahuman level is available. It involves a rat developing and maintaining behavior which keeps him from drowning. A similar demonstration with a young infant is hardly to be proposed; hence the question is likely to remain an academic one.

Partly because of these two considerations, partly because an analysis of infant behavior in terms of operant concepts is still a novel one, and largely because the prevalent method of child study is limited to observation of behavior rather than direct behavioral experimentation, there is very little factual information about the stimuli which function as reinforcers for the young infant. Consequently, our discussion is, to a large extent, speculative.

There are at least two promising leads that may be followed in tentatively identifying stimuli as reinforcers: (1) Stimuli known to be essential to life may prove to be highly effective positive reinforcers, according to experience with infrahuman laboratory organisms. (2) Stimuli which can be demonstrated to function as reinforcers for infrahuman animals and older human subjects, and which do not seem to be acquired reinforcers (Vol. I, pp. 53–58), may reasonably be assumed to function as reinforcers for the young infant as well. Clearly, neither of these approaches is infallible, but, in the absence of experimental data, both seem to provide the most likely basis upon which to organize guesses for present analysis and future research.[1]

SOME PROBABLE REINFORCERS

Food and Water

Food and water are probably the most widely used positive reinforcers in laboratory studies of sub-human operant behavior. These stimuli are essential to life, and they function as reinforcers for virtually every organism studied. Hence it is likely that they also function as positive reinforcers for the human infant. Both food and water come to the young infant as milk. With increasing age, infants are fed milk, water, and a variety of juices separately, and solid food is added to the diet in increasing amounts (roughly corresponding to the emergence of teeth suitable for chewing).

That milk is a *functional* stimulus for infants was established

[1] Although there is little experimental work establishing the reinforcing function of stimuli for infants at present, we believe that this volume is being written at a time marking the imminent performance of such research. We hope that the few studies cited here foretell a flood of demonstrations which will eliminate the need for speculation of this sort.

very clearly by Jensen in 1932. We have described some aspects of Jensen's study in Chapter 3. It is appropriate now to focus on certain aspects of his method, as we did elsewhere (Bijou & Baer, 1960).

> He constructed a special feeding bottle, from which the infant sucked milk; the pressure changes within the bottle arising from each sucking response were transmitted to a kymograph. Milk of the correct temperature (40° C.) gives rise to a steady rate of sucking; variations in the temperature of the milk, or substitution of fluids of differing taste or texture, are reflected in a falling off of the rate or magnitude of response in the same infant. Infants as young as two days old are studied with this method.
>
> Jensen's technique is noteworthy in that it measures a response resulting directly from the stimulus under study. Furthermore, the sucking response is one of the few well-organized and precise responses the newborn has available. This response is easily elicited by all sorts of stimulation, especially in the oral region. Despite this difficulty, the use of a baseline technique in which the infant serves as his own control allows clear conclusions in single cases. The technique would seem worthy of far wider application than it has seen . . . (p. 162).

The study shows that milk (within certain limits of temperature and taste) is functional in controlling the sucking response which ingests it, but it does not distinguish between the eliciting and reinforcing functions of the stimulus. It may be that the milk is acting as a reinforcer, strengthening the sucking response which produces it. On the other hand, it may be that the milk acts as an eliciting stimulus, producing the *next* sucking response rather than reinforcing the *preceding* one. The only modification required to separate these two functions is control of the time when the milk is presented.

Under ordinary circumstances, when the infant sucks, the milk arrives immediately after the suck. If the milk were presented at *random moments* rather than immediately after every suck, and if the sucking response were seen to follow every milk presentation (or nearly every one), the eliciting function of milk as a stimulus would be established. However, if the random presentation of milk did not produce sucking, but milk presented *contingent* upon sucking did increase the rate of sucking, that fact would establish the reinforcing function of milk.

Tactual Stimuli

Some of the most appealing anecdotes in the lore of infant behavior concern the baby's attachment to some blanket, sweater, or Teddy-Bear-like toy. These accounts have in common the clarity of the baby's devotion to the object, the furry or fuzzy nature of the surface of the object, and the baby's behavior of maximizing his body contact with the surface of the object. These components, combined with the near-universal appearance of this phenomenon, lead to the suspicion that certain types of tactual stimulation are positively reinforcing to infants.

In accord with these accounts is the demonstration of the reinforcing function of tactual stimulation for infant monkeys (Harlow, 1948). Harlow conducted a series of studies in which he reared infant monkeys (rhesus macaque) with artificial "mothers." One "mother" consisted of a roll of wire screen for a body, with a head roughly similar to that of a female monkey; for the other "mother" the roll of wire screen was covered with a layer of terrycloth, providing a soft-textured surface. When the infant was clinging to the "wire mother," his tactual stimulation was minimal (and quite possibly aversive); when he was clinging to the "cloth mother," the tactual stimulation was both distinctive and extensive. Both "mothers" were equipped to feed the infant, one or the other making the formula available at all times. The reinforcing function of the tactual stimulation over and above the formula reinforcement was seen in many ways, two of which may be noted: (1) Even though formula was available only from the "wire mother," the infant monkeys spent most of their time clinging to the "cloth mother"; (2) after some weeks in such rearing conditions, the young monkeys were highly sensitive to the sight of the "cloth mother" as a positive reinforcer, and learned a response which produced a momentary view of it.

The conclusion by Harlow that tactual reinforcement is an extremely effective stimulus for the infant monkey should be qualified on the basis of two considerations. One is that the powerful stimulus may possibly involve the sight of the "mother" as well as her feel: The "cloth mother," being solid, has considerably greater resemblance to a true monkey mother than does the transparent "wire mother." It is conceivable (but hardly proven) that the sight of a mother monkey may have reinforcing function for an infant, even one who has had no prior experience with her. The second point is that no attempt was made to capitalize upon the reinforcing power of the food formula, especially when it operated in competition with the tactual (and visual) stimuli provided by the "cloth mother." Were formula to be made available by the "wire mother" only on a schedule—the infant being required to cling to her for increasing lengths of time in order to be fed—it is quite possible that the apparent power of the tactual (and visual) stimuli provided by the "cloth mother" would be reduced. Such questions can be readily resolved by future research.

Harlow's ingenious studies remain a challenging invitation to investigate the role of tactual stimulus functions in much more detail as a mechanism of infant development, and suggest that the infant monkey may prove an excellent subject for such investigations.

Since it is highly probable that tactual stimuli do function as reinforcers for the human infant, a great deal of research along this line lies ahead. The varieties of tactual stimulation are many (as many as the kinds of discriminable surfaces). Common experience suggests that the intensity with which each kind of tactual stimulation acts upon the skin would be a critical factor in determining the direction (positive or negative) of its reinforcing function, if any.

Tactual stimulation could prove extremely important to an understanding of infant development. Because the young infant is largely helpless, he spends a great deal of his time flat against some surface: his bed sheets or blankets, his stroller or infant seat, or his mother. The intensity and extent of tactual stimulation for the infant is thus considerably greater than it is for older children. If such stimulation is reinforcing, then the opportunities for behavioral elaboration through such tactual contingencies are correspondingly great. This is another reason why research in this area seems to have considerable potential.

Sucking-Produced Stimulation

When an infant sucks upon some object, such as a nipple or his own thumb, this act produces a complex of stimulation to his lips, tongue, gums, and the inside surfaces of his cheeks. These tactual and kinesthetic stimuli may have a reinforcing function, as was suggested in the previous section, that is independent of any experience the infant may have had. This possibility often has been postulated, in one set of terms or another (e.g., Levy, 1928).

Whether or not sucking-produced tactual stimuli have a reinforcing function initially in the infant's life, it is inevitable that they will serve as strong acquired reinforcers early in the baby's nursing experiences. Since the baby takes in most of his food by sucking, and since these sucking-produced stimuli are discriminative for anything ingested in this way, they will become *acquired reinforcers.*

Material sucked by a baby ordinarily produces positive reinforcers (in a reasonably well-conducted nursery). But sucking in general will be strengthened by the tactile stimuli it produces, even if at certain times no other reinforcers (food, water) are being taken in. The operation of this process accounts for the appearance of thumb, finger, and even toe sucking; in general, it calls for the sucking of any objects that can be brought to the mouth.

Taste Stimuli

Most objects and liquids which the infant sucks have a taste. The taste alone may well have a reinforcing function, quite apart from the nutritive value of the substance. But, just like sucking-produced tactual and kinesthetic stimuli, taste stimuli should soon acquire a reinforcing function, if they do not already have one. Sweet and salty tastes are discriminative stimuli for the ingestion of many foods given to the infant. If these foods are positive reinforcers, then their taste stimuli should acquire durable positive reinforcing functions.

Jensen's study (described above) showed that solutions of sweet or salty substances would support sucking, but that acid tastes would not. It was also apparent that high concentrations of salt stopped the sucking response completely, and that some lesser concentrations of sweet and salty substances would support more sucking than others. Other studies (Pratt, Nelson, & Sun, 1930) have shown general changes in the activity of young infants when an applicator, dipped in various solutions, was placed in the mouth. Sucking responses appeared often for sweet or salty tastes, but rarely for sour (acid) or bitter (quinine) solutions. Other common responses to sour and bitter tastes were facial grimaces and ejecting tongue movements. These observations hardly establish taste stimuli as reinforcing, but they do strongly indicate that these stimuli have some function which may well be a reinforcing one (positive in the case of sweet and salty tastes, negative in the case of sour and bitter, within fairly wide limits of concentration).

If the taste property of a stimulus functions as a reinforcer, it would augment the reinforcing value of certain foods and reduce the reinforcing value of others. In the same way, the taste property of objects other than foods would add to or subtract from the reinforcement produced by sucking on them.

It might be that certain chemicals applied to the tongue are more effective reinforcers than the nutritive components of food independent of their tastes, and that food serves as a reinforcer mainly because of its taste properties. There is a body of experimental literature bearing on this possibility, using animals as subjects. The data so far do not resolve the question, even at the animal level, and therefore generalization to the human infant is highly speculative. We note only the possibilities for future reference.

Skin Temperature

The internal temperature of the infant's body is fairly well regulated by homeostatic biological mechanisms; the temperatures which act upon his skin, however, are a matter of environmental happenstance. With infrahuman animals, it may be shown that too high or too low temperatures act as negative reinforcers, and strengthen behavior which changes them. With human adults we note the everyday patterns of behavior which are obviously supported by the temperature changes they produce: in warm settings, we turn on fans and air-conditioners, open windows, remove excessive clothing, and go swimming; in cold situations, we add sweaters, coats, and gloves, close windows, adjust thermostats, pile blankets on our beds, and gather about fires. (There may be reinforcers other than temperature to be secured or avoided by these behaviors, of course, but the role of temperature in each is clear.)

It is a fair assumption that babies, too, are sensitive to fluctuations in skin temperature as reinforcing stimulus operations. The laboratory evidence available demonstrates merely that high or low temperatures (16° or 45° C.) applied to the skin produce changes in the infant's general activity level (e.g., Crudden, 1937). A demonstration that operant behavior could be strengthened by a shift from such extremes back to body temperature (37° C.) is not available. It would not seem to be a more difficult observation to arrange than others already accomplished.

There are a number of stimuli frequently associated with temperature changes. Notable among these is the baby's crib blanket. It is continuously present as the baby gradually warms under it; its continued absence marks a time of gradual cooling, in a cool room. The slowness of the change might not prevent a discriminated reaction to this stimulus. Since stimuli which are discriminative for other reinforcers acquire a reinforcing function (Vol. I, pp. 54–58), and if the temperature changes referred to here are reinforcing to the infant, then the blanket (and other objects such as sleepers and sweaters) may well take on positive reinforcing value.

Rest and Sleep

Any parent can testify that a tired baby is irritable, easily moved to crying, and in many other ways different from when he is rested. These observations lead to the guess that lack of rest or sleep is a *setting event*, lowering the threshold of elicitation of a number of emotional respondents involved in crying and fussing, and altering a number of discriminated operants as well (the tired child may not "mind" his parents, may not "remember" the few words he knows, may be aggressive toward his siblings, etc.).

An interesting question arises: Does the cumulation of fatigue or the lack of sleep make a positive reinforcer of rest and sleep? It may be shown that when the adult is deprived of rest, the opportunity to rest becomes a positive reinforcer and will strengthen any response leading to such a possibility. Thus, a man turning a handwheel against a friction clutch will show an increase in wheel-turning behavior when given a longer rest period at the end of a specified number of revolutions of the handwheel (Azrin, 1960).

It is a fair assumption that rest and sleep operate as reinforcers for the infant. It has been estimated that the newborn sleeps about 83% of the time (Pratt, Nelson, & Sun, 1930). Hence it may well be true that he is easily deprived of sleep, especially when a busy mother, for lack of a babysitter, finds it necessary to take the baby on her many daily errands, a situation which is bound to be disruptive to the baby's sleep routine. (Some infants fall asleep anywhere: grocery carts, strollers, store counters, etc.; most infants, however, are rather easily kept awake.)

A number of stimuli could be closely associated with the onset of sleep and could thereby become functional. Some of these are social, involving the mother who commonly prepares the child for bed and "puts him to sleep." These will be considered in Chapter 8. Others are physical stimuli: the crib in which the child sleeps, the toys, Teddy Bears, or dolls consistently kept in his crib as sleeping companions, the special clothes the infant sleeps in, and, notably, the blanket. These objects often are arranged so that they readily become discriminative for rest and sleep. If stimuli produced by rest are positive reinforcers, then the social and physical stimuli described above acquire positive reinforcing functions, according to the principle of acquired reinforcement (Vol. I, pp. 54–58). We now consider the crib blanket as a special case.

The Blanket: A Generalized Reinforcer

Skinner (1953) describes the generalized reinforcer as a conditional reinforcer which has been paired with more than one primary reinforcer, and therefore may prove highly persistent in its acquired reinforcing function, because the momentary condition of the organism is not very important. The blanket may be analyzed as developing a generalized reinforcing function for many babies.

The blanket has entered our account of infant development in three ways: (1) It can be discriminative for skin temperature changes of a positively reinforcing sort. (2) It can be discriminative for rest and sleep which may be positively reinforcing. (3) It can be a source of extensive tactual stimulation which may be positively reinforcing, particularly since baby blankets are designed to have a soft and pleasing surface (i.e., it may serve as an ecological reinforcer).

All three of these roles combine in establishing the blanket as a positively reinforcing stimulus in its own right. Under these circumstances the blanket, in all probability, becomes one of the baby's first generalized reinforcers.

These are numerous anecdotes which seem to support the identification of blankets as powerful reinforcers for infants.[2] Many parents tell of their baby's becoming attached to his blanket, hardly being able to sleep without it (and often sleeping on it rather than under it, especially in warm weather), frequently carrying it about with him, even hugging it on occasion. The persistence of such observations has led to the term "security" blanket. It is simpler to point to the generalized status of the blanket as discriminative for a number of reinforcing stimuli than to assess it as a source of security.

Opportunity to Breathe

We have noted previously that a demonstration of the reinforcing function of the opportunity to breathe is available at the infrahuman level. It is obvious that human adults, in learning to swim, also learn a chain of head, neck, mouth, and breathing responses tightly reinforced by this stimulus, air going into the nose and mouth. Thus it is a strong assumption that this stimulus is an effective positive reinforcer for infants.

Its role in infant development appears to be trivial, however. The infant very rarely is deprived of an opportunity to breathe. The exceptions to this are respiratory illnesses and accidental pro-

[2] The reader should note that "anecdotes" are not as reliable as experimental data, and that to support a claim by informal accounts is not as dependable as experimental demonstration.

longed covering of the nose and mouth. It is conceivable that in such situations, response chains involving neck and trunk muscles which free the head, or other responses which move the bedclothes and pillows, may have some small reinforcement by improving the opportunity to breathe, and thus coordination of the body may be improved a trifle. It is difficult to imagine that this is a frequent learning experience for infants.[3]

Negative Reinforcers

Negative reinforcers are sometimes referred to as stimuli which cause pain. Pain is a highly subjective concept, being most meaningful for the person experiencing it. Observers usually infer that there is pain in another by the subject's verbal statement that something hurts, by his facial grimaces or body contortions, or by the observers' own past experiences: they would hurt, they say, if they were in that same stimulus situation. Unfortunately, these indicators of pain are not reliable.

Verbal statements as criteria for pain may be false, as in lying and malingering. Hence verbal responses, rather than reflecting the presence of actual negative reinforcers, may be made because they produce other positive reinforcers: a rest in bed, or money from an insurance company, for example. Or, statements of pain may be used to avoid other reinforcers, such as going to school or hard work. And the facial and body contortions of pain are often seen on occasions of a bad pun or an inept artistic performance, for example, as well as on occasions of painful physical stimulation.

Assuming that someone else is in pain because in a similar situation we would be, imputes our own thresholds of stimulation to others, as well as our own training in endurance and the usual

[3] Modern technology has provided almost every household with a variety of pieces of light, clinging plastic wrapping. Occasional tragic interactions between infants and such plastic have different outcomes than we have just described: the plastic clings so effectively to the face of the child that breathing is impossible, not merely restricted, and strangulation can occur before the child's own responses free his face or a rescuer appears, for the child has only a moment. Not all reinforcement contingencies teach.

consequences of that stimulation. (We, for example, may find needle pricks painful; a narcotics addict may not.)

These examples represent adult behaviors rather than infant behaviors, and are highly influenced by patterns of experience not yet encountered by an infant. "Pain" is an adult's word; children must be taught to use it as a label for certain respondents like crying, for situations which their teachers think to be painful, and for situations in which the child displays avoidance behavior.

The concept of the negative reinforcer therefore has many advantages over the concept of pain: If a stimulus can be used to strengthen behaviors which escape or avoid it, we can call that stimulus by its functional designation—a negative reinforcer. We can also call it painful if we like, but we gain nothing except two labels for one phenomenon, and may add confusion rather than clarification to a systematic analysis.

The human adult is sensitive to a large number of physical, chemical, and organismic stimuli which function as negative reinforcers. Many of these do not appear to be acquired reinforcers; so we may guess that the infant is also sensitive to them. To list them all would be idle; fortunately, they can be discussed in fairly objective terms with respect to their intensity.

Almost any stimulus dimension to which one is sensitive can be made negatively reinforcing by presenting it in sufficient intensity. Thus, bright light, loud sounds, high temperatures, strong pressure, sudden and rapid stimulus change, and highly concentrated solutions of certain chemicals (acids, bases, and some tastes and smells) are commonly avoided.

The category of high pressures is interesting because of its complexity. Pressure, as a physical event, is a result of force applied over an area. A rather small force can produce a great pressure if applied to a very small area. If the area is the skin of an infant, then a number of devices can be thought of as applying modest forces to small areas: pins, edges and corners of blocks and toys, shoes, string, etc. The infant's own muscles often supply the force in considerable magnitude, as when he bangs his head and arms against walls and floors. Pressures may occur within the child as well: the fretful behavior of an infant with a bubble of air trapped in his stomach is one of the classics of childrearing lore, as is the magical stopping of that fussing immediately following the belch which frees it.

The infant's world is usually designed by his parents to preclude his encountering the most extreme forms of negative reinforcers. Nevertheless, as the previous examples suggest, the ordinary experiences of an infant include frequent meetings with moderate intensities of these stimuli. Consequently, behavior chains which avoid and escape from these stimuli develop, contributing to the steadily increasing efficiency and skill of the baby in the use of his body. In the same way, clumsy responses with objects are weakened, as they present such negative reinforcers. This, too, is a contribution to skill. For example, a child rolling a large truck about on the floor is in a situation to roll it over his own fingers. Were this to happen, his own weight pressing on the truck as he pushes could exert considerable pressure on his fingers. The responses leading to this outcome would then be weakened. The result of a number of such occurrences probably would be a pattern of play with this toy which resulted in keeping the fingers out from under the truck's wheels as it was pushed along. We would say that the child's subsequent performance with the truck was more skillful, if only because it was marked by fewer crying episodes.

SOME SPECULATIVE REINFORCERS

General Stimulus Change

Some laboratory studies of infrahuman subjects suggest that almost any stimulus change can be reinforcing under certain conditions. The flashing of a light, the clicking of a switch, the movement of an object: these are stimulus events which, by themselves, rarely show reinforcing functions. However, if an animal is placed in a highly restrictive environment where he can do very little; if, in addition, few stimulus changes are allowed to occur; and if time is allowed to pass under these circumstances, then it is possible to find that a response which consistently produces a light flash, or a click, or a movement, is strengthened thereby.

By progressively restricting the movements of the animal, stimulus change produced by his own behavior is correspondingly reduced. If changes in external stimuli are kept to a minimum, and time passes under these conditions, then it could be said that a deprivation of stimulus variability is taking place. If stimulus change in general is a reinforcer, it is a relatively weak one: its behavior-strengthening property seems modest at best, and then only under conditions of extreme deprivation for stimulus change.

A similar phenomenon can be demonstrated in adults. Common experience suggests that in a state of boredom (which has an obvious relationship to deprivation of stimulus change), an adult may engage in behavior which has very casual stimulus consequences, but which nevertheless produces some stimulus change: twiddling his thumbs, drumming his fingertips on a table, whistling, pacing, talking to himself, working a retractible ball-point pen, etc. These behaviors are not particularly strong. It is a matter of interpretation to view them as supported by the stimulus change they produce.

To extend this principle to the infant requires the assumption that he, too, can be deprived of stimulus change with the same consequences as in infrahuman animals and human adults. It is to be noted that a good deal of an infant's time is spent in relatively quiet and uneventful environments, especially in the first months after birth. In large part, this is due to the fact that the infant spends between 65 and 80 percent of his first days asleep, this proportion shifting only gradually with increasing age toward the 33 percent characteristic of adults. Most parents attempt to provide a quiet situation for the baby's slumber. The infant awakening in such a protective environment thus may be subjected to a period without much stimulus change, until his parents discover that he is awake and move him to the kitchen or some other room where many exciting things are happening.

If stimulus change in general is considered as a potentially reinforcing stimulus function for infants, then it would seem that almost any variety of behaviors would be strengthened by it, since virtually any responses accomplish stimulus change, if only of a kinesthetic sort. Some behaviors, however, produce more obvious, prominent, or intense stimulus changes than others. These behaviors should be strengthened more, all other factors being equal. On the other hand, those behaviors which produce the more noticeable stimulus changes often will be the more effortful responses of the infant's repertory. The effortfulness of a response may serve as a negative reinforcer (Keller & Schoenfeld, 1950). If it does it would be expected that more effortful responses would be weakened relative to other, less effortful responses accomplishing the same end.

Thus an infant patting the floor with his hand may produce a soft slapping sound, which, acting simply as stimulus change, could serve to strengthen the response to a modest degree. A more energetic pat would produce a more prominent stimulus change (a louder sound and a more distinctive tactual stimulation to the baby's palm). But it would also require more effort. The former consequences could serve to strengthen the response more effectively. The latter could weaken it. An even more energetic response by the infant obviously could be aversive to the palm of his hand. How these two contradictory stimulus functions interact to strengthen, weaken, or leave unchanged the behaviors that produce them cannot be settled by deduction. It will take a great deal of experimental manipulation, both of the magnitude of the stimulus change produced by a response and of the effort inherent in that response, before the contribution of these possible dimensions to infant development can be stated accurately and comprehensively. One of the most promising beginnings of a program of this sort is the work of Rheingold, Stanley, and Cooley (1960).

These investigators studied six-month-old infants in a situation where a casual response by the baby could produce a marked change in the color and movement of a visual display. The infant was placed in a seat specially designed to support his weight and hold him so that a large movie screen immediately before him could be easily seen. A metal sphere was mounted in front of the child, almost in his lap, so that he could easily contact the sphere by minimal motions of either arm or hand. During the experimental sessions, such responses (detected by a special electronic device) activated a motion picture projector which cast a moving display of brightly colored geometric forms on the screen before the infant. This stimulus consequence increased the frequency of sphere-contacting behavior during at least some experimental sessions.

Rheingold and her associates utilized an experimental procedure that evaluated the role of the temporal relationships between the stimuli and responses involved. They included in their observations conditions in which the stimulus display changed at random movements, not contingent on the infant's responding. Under these conditions, the touching response was not strengthened as much as it was during contingent stimulus changes. This finding showed that the visual stimulus change functioned as a reinforcer of a sphere-touching behavior producing it, rather than as an eliciting, discriminative, or "exciting" stimulus (a term some psychologists prefer) leading to generally increased behavior by the baby. Information of this sort contributes significantly to a determination of what constitutes a reinforcing stimulus for infants.

Control of the Environment

It has often been thought that power is profoundly valuable to humans. Adler (1927), arguing in the spirit of Freud's principles of psychology, claimed that an urge to gain and exercise power was a fundamental human instinct. Skinner (1953) remarked that children "play for hours with mechanical toys, paints, scissors and paper, noise-makers, puzzles—in short, with almost anything which feeds back significant changes in the environment and is reasonably free of aversive properties. The sheer control of nature is itself reinforcing." It is possible to derive this same principle of behavior from the early development of infants in relation to the physical and organismic stimuli. The argument, it should be emphasized, is deductive, not experimentally derived.

A large class of changes in behavior to physical stimuli are a matter of increases in coordinated chains of more and more complex motor responses, i.e., a matter of behavioral elaboration. These behaviors are the ones which manipulate the environment to produce reinforcing outcomes. Some performances succeed very well in doing this, others succeed only moderately well, and still others fail. Behaviors which succeed are considered skillful;

those which fail are viewed as clumsy. If the skillfulness itself produces a pattern of proprioceptive stimuli, then that pattern could be a discriminative stimulus associated with positive reinforcers and avoiding negative ones. Similarly, if the clumsiness itself produces a pattern of such stimuli, that pattern could be a discriminative stimulus for the loss of positive reinforcers, the continued presence of negative reinforcers, or the presentation of new negative reinforcers. Then skillfulness and clumsiness would acquire reinforcing functions. Skillfulness would acquire a positive reinforcing function, and clumsiness a negative reinforcing function.

In these situations, behaviors which are skillful would be self-reinforcing; behaviors which are clumsy would be self-punishing. In other words, skillful behaviors would grow steadily in strength, and clumsy ones would become weak, by virtue of their own inherent characteristics, and independently of any other reinforcers they may produce or avoid. Such self-reinforcement has the great advantage of operating within chains, and then *just* at the moment when they can do the most good. The baby then would display skillful behaviors on many occasions when these behaviors accomplish nothing other than their own action—he should "play" with his environment. By playing with it, he displays skill: he displays control of his environment, making it work, move, be held, be still, make noises, make sounds—in effect, be his to make function.

For example, the child who manipulates food sufficiently well to get it to his mouth is, in the process, developing skill in the control of stimuli which are discriminative for the eating. As he picks up a piece of food to bring it to his mouth, he sets the stage for either success or failure. A poor performance with his fingers drops the food or crushes it; a skillful performance keeps the food in the fingers, undamaged, until the hand brings that food to the proper place and produces reinforcement. The stimuli most prominently discriminative for this reinforcement are the sight of the food between the fingers and the feel of it there, as the hand begins to bring the food toward the body. There will come a point when his view of this spectacle is cut off, but the tactual stimulation provided by the object will remain until the food is released in the mouth. Were the baby to drop the food, the sight and the sudden cessation of the feel of the object would be discriminative for chain breaking and nonreinforcement. Thus, the sight and feel of an object successfully held acquire positive reinforcing functions. Behaviors which in the future succeed in holding an object (not necessarily food) will be strengthened by these acquired reinforcers. And, indeed, the holding of otherwise useless objects for long periods is a prominent characteristic of infants.

Returning to the example, as the infant successfully brings food to his mouth, he presents to himself the sight and feel of a held object *moving through space.* This motion too is a stimulus dimension which becomes discriminative for the reinforcement provided by eating the food and also acquires a positive reinforcing function. Thus, in the future, classes of behaviors which move held objects through space and terminate in reinforcement will be strengthened thereby. Another prominent behavior of young children is the waving about of their toys, "aimlessly" to the eye of an observer.

These examples only suggest the ways in which control of his environment[4] signals imminent reinforcement for the infant. Movements of the fingers, hands, arms, legs, trunk, eyes, vocal cords, and the whole body often will be involved in such contingencies. Thus behaviors which, in the future, achieve similar sorts of control over nonreinforcing objects will be reinforced nevertheless not by the objects, but by their control of these objects. The normal baby could be one who is manipulative, exploratory, and curious. He will tinker with things, take them apart, carry them

[4] These examples should do much to limit the meaning of "control" in this discussion. It is perhaps unfortunate that "control," a logical word for this stimulus dimension, should have so many meanings in everyday language. Let it be emphasized that "control" here refers to the stimulus dimensions involved in skillful and successful performances of various parts of the child's body, as the above examples portray. It is an extension of the idea of skill in the use of a tool, instrument, technique, or artistic medium. We are not referring to the idea of self-control (which we have discussed somewhat differently in Volume I, pp. 76–82), nor to the concept of authoritarian or political control in the sense of force or tyranny, nor to the much-honored practices of experimental control in scientific research, nor to the technical concept of "stimulus control" as used by learning theorists.

about, tap them together, and stack them. If an object works in some way, as a door latch or a switch or a spring works, he will manipulate it. If a new place is discovered, he will enter it and walk around in it in many ways and from many directions. If there is available a vehicle which can move him about faster and more effortlessly than he can walk, he will move in that vehicle, often for no other reason than to be moving. In short, he will control his environment because the control itself is reinforcing: it has been consistently discriminative for the addition of positive reinforcers and the avoidance of negative ones.

It is conceivable, of course, that control of the environment functions as a reinforcer without such a history. Even were this demonstrated, it would not alter the preceding analysis. It would be virtually impossible to avoid experiencing contingencies in which control of the environment is discriminative for other reinforcement; therefore, a steady increase in the reinforcing value of control of environmental stimuli will result, whether the initial reinforcing value of such control is zero or greater. This point has been made before, as in sucking-produced stimuli (stimuli produced by sucking), and will be referred to again in Chapter 8 in the analysis of social reinforcers—attention, approval, and affection.

Control of the environment is not identical as a reinforcer with general stimulus change. The first difference is that clumsy, awkward behaviors often provide clear-cut stimulus changes, as when a heavy object slips from the fingers and falls to the floor. If stimulus change were the sole reinforcer, clumsy behaviors would grow in strength equally or possible more so. To identify control of the environment as a reinforcer suggests, however, that skillful behaviors will grow in strength more than clumsy ones.

The second difference is that stimulus change seems more dependent upon deprivation for its reinforcing strength than does control of the environment. Control of the environment, too, would seem to be sensitive to deprivation, such that if periods went by when most responses failed or were clumsy, then the reinforcing effectiveness of a skillful performance well might be increased. But even without such periods of deprivation, control of the environment seems to have its reinforcing effect: infants play for long periods with apparently nonreinforcing objects, their skillful behaviors steadily increasing, their clumsy responses steadily decreasing, unless other stimulating and setting conditions are operating.

Should the study by Rheingold, Stanley, and Cooley (1962) be interpreted as a demonstration of the reinforcing value of stimulus change or the reinforcing value of control of the environment for those infants? We cannot say. Obviously, the behavior of the babies produced both consequences. This interrelationship is perhaps the major difficulty in these analyses. General stimulus change and control of the environment are not simple physical or kinesthetic stimulus events. They are instead broad classes of such stimuli, which have in common certain functional properties according to a systematic logic. The logic may appear sound, but if it does not take into account the relevant principles of behavior simultaneously, it may easily lead to a wrong conclusion.

Only a series of experimental studies can show the strengths and weaknesses of these analyses. It should be clear that such demonstrations will be difficult to accomplish. Since the stimuli in question are broad classes rather than a group of discrete events, experiments with these classes must be correspondingly numerous and varied. In addition, these stimuli, even in single examples, may prove difficult to manipulate experimentally. How do we provide an environment in which control of it is *not* discriminative for other reinforcers, for example? Could we consider rearing a child in an environment in which only *clumsy* responses will produce positive reinforcers and avoid negative ones?

These concepts are worth considering, even if they prove difficult to validate through experimental demonstration. For one thing, the research needed to clarify them, while complicated, may not prove impossible to conduct. New techniques and technologies can be expected to facilitate the task. For another, these ideas may well be sound. If so, they are basic processes of child development, explaining much of the competence of adults to deal with their physical, chemical, and organismic world.

REFERENCES

Adler, A. *The practice and theory of individual psychology.* New York: Harcourt, 1927.

Azrin, N. H. Use of rests as reinforcers. *Psychol. Reports,* 1960, *7,* 240.

Bijou, S. W., & Baer, D. M. The laboratory-experimental study of child behavior. In P. H. Mussen (Ed.), *Handbook of research methods in child development.* New York: Wiley, 1960.

Crudden, C. H. Reactions of newborn infants to thermal stimuli under constant tactual conditions. *J. exp. Psychol.,* 1937, *20,* 350–370.

Harlow, H. F. The nature of love. *Amer. Psychologist,* 1958, *13,* 673–685.

Jensen, K. Differential reactions to taste and temperature stimuli in newborn infants. *Genet. Psychol. Monogr.,* 1932, *12,* 361–479.

Keller, F. S., & Schoenfeld, W. N. *Principles of psychology.* New York: Appleton-Century-Crofts, 1950.

Levy, D. M. Fingersucking and accessory movements in early infancy: an etiological study. *Amer. J. Psychiat.,* 1928, *7,* 881–918.

Pratt, K. C., Nelson, Amalie K., & Sun, K. H. *The behavior of the newborn infant.* Columbus: Ohio State Univer. Press, 1930.

Rheingold, Harriet L., Stanley, W. C., & Cooley, J. A. A crib for the study of exploratory behavior in infants. *Science,* 1962, *136,* 1054–1055.

Skinner, B. F. The science of learning and the art of teaching. *Cumulative record.* New York: Appleton-Century-Crofts, 1953.

7

Initial Formation of Manual and Locomotor Dexterity

One of the most interesting aspects of infant development is the change that takes place in the *form* of behavior as the early, uncoordinated and ineffective responses of the infant are steadily refined into increasingly numerous, skillful, and effective behaviors. From a parent's point of view, this phase of development is not only delightful to observe, but is often a significant token of the child's health and excellence and is consistently evaluated as a promise of adult character.

Developmental psychologists unromantically refer to the process as motor development and examine the course of this development for an understanding of the processes involved. Many point out that motor development consists not only of the evolution and maintenance of certain classes of increasingly complex responses, but also of the simultaneous weakening of other responses. For example, as the four-and-a-half-month-old infant learns to grasp a rattle, he displays a great deal of vigorous kicking. With repeated presentations of the rattle not only does the grasp response become more efficient but the accompanying kicking behavior drops to practically zero (Curti, 1930).

Since the course of motor development is usually viewed as an unfolding process, observations of sequences as attainment of grasp responses prove progress, and erect posture and locomotion have led to the establishment of norms—average ages at which nameable classes of motor responses may be said to appear. Detailed accounts of a wide range of motor norms on populations of infants in this country may be found in most textbooks on child psychology (e.g., Hurlock, 1964; Munn, 1951; and Thompson, 1962).

Motor development may, of course, be studied also for the purpose of determining the conditions (organismic, physical, and social) that shape and maintain motor behavior. One such approach and the one followed here views motor development as a complex of operant interactions. Motor development is analyzed here in terms of three-form formulas involving discriminative stimuli, differentiated responses, and reinforcing consequences.

We have already examined many of the relationships holding among reinforcing and discriminative stimuli (Chapters 5 and 6). We shall now concentrate on the responses and their changes in form.

In the literature of child development, motor development is recognized as taking place as much in the acquisition of simple skills, such as reaching accurately for an object seen, as it is in the later building of repertories as elaborate as playing the piano with virtuosity. Both examples are frequently cited as testimony to the predominating role of biological variables. That is, since almost every child learns to reach accurately for objects, this skill is characterized as a universal inheritance of the species which naturally and inevitably unfolds during the course of growth. On the other hand, since few people become accomplished pianists, the feat of playing the piano with competence is thought of as requiring a rare talent with which one must be born. We will examine each of these skills in some detail in this chapter to analyze their interactional roots.

Consider for a moment the role of biological and inherited characteristics in motor development. The *biological structure* of the child obviously contributes to the possibility of certain responses in his behavior. The possession of legs and feet makes possible a variety of locomotor responses, fingers allow for a wealth of manipulation behavior, and a flexible and facile tongue permits a modest variation of sounds. In addition, motor development is influenced to a certain degree by *biological functioning*. Behavior is stimulated by a shortage of food within the biological system which gives rise to stimulation called hunger; an abundance of adrenalin in the biological system produces "uneasiness," and so on.

Biological structural and functional differences between individual infants are not critical to this discussion, nor are the differences in maturational rates, since both are ordinarily minor in the total course of motor development. The species determined biological characteristics to motor development, set gross limitations on the final forms, shapes, and styles of behavior.

The major contributions to motor development originate in the interaction between the biological structure and the stimulus antecedents and consequences of the behaviors they make possible. In this chapter, we are interested primarily in the fine form and detail of motor development; so our emphasis is mainly on the process of differentiation and discrimination of operants in both short and long chains.

MANUAL DEXTERITY

In order to illustrate the foregoing points, we begin our discussion by examining the acquisition of manual dexterity. Certainly piano playing is an example of highly complex behavior involving manual dexterity. What are some of the behaviors which must be developed before one can acquire these?

First of all, the performer must be able to sit before the piano in a position that enables him to perform the other necessary responses. This apparently simple feat in itself represents a complex interplay of muscular responses in the trunk and legs of the performer, discriminated to the kinesthetic stimuli produced by the motions of the muscles, to tactual stimuli arising from the chair on which the performer sits, and to internal stimuli arising in the semi-circular canals of the inner ear, which provide cues for balancing the body.

Second, the arms will have to maintain the hands at a certain height so that the fingers may play upon the keys properly. This response can be controlled by discriminative stimuli produced in the shoulder and arm muscles as they maintain tonus to keep the arms elevated, and by tactual stimuli arising from the finger tips as they rest or press on the keys.

Finally, the piano playing itself centers about a sequence of finger movements on the keys of the piano, movements that call for separate finger action or a combination of finger actions, for a range of effort in depressing the keys to produce various tones, and for great dexterity of the fingers in moving up and down the keyboard to produce the desired sounds.

The movement of the fingers is under the control of many discriminative stimuli, of which the most prominent are the printed notes before the player and the location of the keys on the piano.

Since the player must learn to look at the music instead of the keys, discriminative control is exerted by kinesthetic stimuli arising from the position of the hands and fingers rather than from the sight of the hands. Furthermore, any finger must be able to strike any key.

A certain interval of time must separate finger motions. Thus, at least two more discriminative stimuli are involved, the visual form of the notes defining their time value (whole notes, eighths, etc.) and the passage of time.

If the performer is beating out the time with his foot, the motions of his foot produce a pattern of kinesthetic stimuli which are discriminative for the moments when the finger motions should occur. Furthermore, the beating of the foot is controlled by the passing of time or by the spoken word (*one*, two three; *one*, two three) or by the clicking of a metronome.

The motions of the arm, too, are controlled by the visual stimuli on the printed page, this time by the relative position of the notes on the scale, properly cued to the 88 keys of the piano. The arm motions must also come under the control of kinesthetic stimuli produced by the finger motions which they support.

Thus, many skills are involved in piano playing. A young infant does not play the piano. However, he does move his fingers in a way which could depress piano keys; he does move his arms in ways which could bring his hands from one portion of the keyboard to another; he does show motions of his feet which are like the motions used to beat time; he does show contractions of the trunk and other muscles which could support his weight in a sitting position; and he does move his eyes in a tracking manner which could allow him to scan a line of music.

The environments of all infants teach them the major part of the response classes involved in piano playing; this basic instruction begins immediately after birth. It is only the *final organization* of these responses that is optional and that determines which child plays the piano and which does not. Indeed, many complex motor performances practiced by adults (of which piano playing is only an arbitrary example) have their roots in early environmental differentiation and discrimination of the gross, imprecise, and typically unnamed operant behaviors of the young infant.

As to how early an infant could learn to play the piano, there are several factors to consider. Most skills must be learned in sequences, the more basic ones being prerequisites for the more advanced. Since no one has yet designed a sophisticated environment deliberately aimed at developing piano playing in an infant, it would be difficult to say how soon this could be accomplished. The important point is that the actual playing of the piano is a matter of highly differentiated and chained sequences of already existing behaviors. The physical environment instructs infants in the majority of the skills necessary for this performance.

To examine in detail the roots of one of the skills in which the environment normally and somewhat automatically instructs the infant, we will consider separate finger responses. The very young infant does not usually show separate finger responses. His hand movements involve a simultaneous flexing of all his fingers, showing either an open hand or, more frequently, a closed fist. To differentiate separate finger responses requires an environment in which different reinforcement contingencies operate for movements of one finger than operate for movements of more than one.

A pea on a table top is an example of such an environment. Attempts to pick up the pea by scooping it into the palm with all five fingers succeed only occasionally and after considerable time and effort, but attempts to pick up the pea with a scissor movement of the thumb and forefinger are likely to succeed more frequently and more easily. A pea in the mouth will function as a positive reinforcer for a young infant; hence this situation exemplifies the general procedures for accomplishing response differentiation (Vol. I, pp. 52–53). This kind of experience can in principle separate total hand responses into independent finger actions.

By contrast, a hard-boiled egg (shelled) on that same table top constitutes an environment in which simultaneous flexion of all or most of the fingers will continue to be the only response pattern that allows the child to manipulate the egg successfully. The size of most eggs is such that a thumb and forefinger grasp will not produce enough grip on the slippery egg to hold it, but a more thorough encompassing of it by four or five fingers will.

Too light a grip by the fingers on the egg will lose it, and too tight a grip will reduce it to debris not easily eaten. Similarly, if thumb and forefinger grasp a pea with too little force, the pea will fall. If the grasp involves too much force, the pea will be crushed, and may be lost or no longer constitute a reinforcing stimulus to the infant. Thus the pea and egg also constitute environments which can differentiate various levels of strength of both separate and coordinated finger responses.

These examples may be readily generalized. The physical world obviously contains many objects which shape the child's skills with hands and fingers, simply because they defy manipulation until the right combination of finger movements of suitable force is applied. So long as that manipulation produces some sort of reinforcing stimulus consequences for the infant at the end of the finger-movement chain (such as eating the pea and the egg), the differentiation of these finger responses will take place.

This differentiation into chains of stimulus-response units could hardly fail to come under the control of discriminative stimuli (Vol. I, pp. 48–52). By way of example, consider the infant sitting in a baby table with one pea on the table before him. Let us say that peas are positive reinforcers for this infant, and that peas have been discriminative for eating behaviors. Hence the sight of the pea will serve to attract and hold the infant's attention. If the infant reaches for the pea, he is starting a chain of trunk, arm, hand, and finger responses. That is, he leans forward, contracting stomach muscles and relaxing back muscles; his arm reaches forward, involving triceps flexion and biceps relaxation; muscles in the forearm contract to open his hand; other muscles then will contract to close finger and thumb about the pea; the arm muscles will reverse their action to bring the hand back from the table and toward the mouth; upon reaching the mouth the hand must insert the thumb and forefinger into the mouth and then relax its grip on the pea. The chain ends in reinforcement, which serves to strengthen the entire chain antecedent to this reinforcement.

However, there is virtually an infinite class of such object-reaching chains. Of these, only some will result in the capturing of the pea; the others bring the hand to rest not on the pea but elsewhere on the table top. Those chains which result in the child's capturing the pea are reinforced; those which result in missing the pea are not. The successful chains should grow in strength as a result of this reinforcement; the unsuccessful ones extinguish. But a chain which results in the capturing of a pea in one spot on the table may fail when the pea is placed in a different spot; and a chain which fails for the first location of the pea may be exactly the one which succeeds for the second location of the pea. Obviously, skillful behavior consists of both chains; one discriminated to the first location, and the other to the second. That is, Chain #1 should be strong for Pea Location #1, but weak for Pea Location #2; Chain #2 should have the reverse characteristics.

The process of discrimination accomplishes just that. *The strengthening of responses or chains of responses is specific to the stimulus situations in which reinforcement takes place; the weakening of responses or chains of responses is specific to the stimulus situations in which punishment or extinction takes place* (Vol. I, pp. 51–52).

The stimulus situations in which the chains discussed above either produce reinforcement or extinction are rich in the number and variety of stimuli. There are visual components, prominent among which are the sight of the pea on the table, and the sight of the hands relative to the pea and the table. To look at the pea and his hands, the child moves his eyes so as to fixate upon objects and executes just enough binocular convergence to produce a fused image from the two retinal projections. Kinesthetic stimulation arising from these visual responses also contributes to the stimulus situation. Furthermore, there is a large class of kinesthetic stimulation provided by the position of the child's body, especially the position of the arm and hand in reaching.

All these stimuli (plus others we need not list here) serve as discriminative stimuli, marking an occasion on which certain chains will produce reinforcement while others will not. Those responses that do produce reinforcement become stronger in *that* total stimulus situation; those responses that fail to produce reinforcement become weaker, again in *that* total stimulus situation. In a different stimulus situation, these strengths and weaknesses will not be apparent, but another set will. It will be the set that has resulted from the patterns of reinforcement and extinction characteristic of that different stimulus situation.

Furthermore, the stimulus situations within which response chains take place are systematically changed by the chain as it proceeds. At the beginning of a successful reach for the pea, the infant is responding to a complex of visual and kinesthetic stimuli which in the past have set the occasion for the specific lean forward and arm extension that he now is displaying. But as the lean and the arm extension proceed, a stimulus change is automatically produced by these responses: the pea now casts a larger projection on the retina, and the angle of convergence of the eyes is greater in maintaining a fused image; the tension of the stomach muscles is greater, as is the extension of the back muscles; similarly, the pattern of tension in the biceps and triceps of the arm has changed; and the sight of the arm, extended in front of the child, is somewhat different from what it was a moment before. This new stimulus situation, slightly changed from the preceding one, is the discriminative stimulus for the next response in the chain: further extension of the arm, a bit more lean forward, and the opposing of thumb and forefinger around the pea.

As the chain proceeds, it still further alters the stimulus situation, producing still different patterns of strain and relaxation in the muscles, different patterns of visual stimulation, retinal image, and binocular convergence, and an entirely new tactual stimulation from the pea against fingertip and thumb. This new pattern is discriminative for a certain strength of grip by finger and thumb and for a reversing pattern of arm and trunk muscle action. The arm now begins to flex, biceps contracting and triceps relaxing, so that the hand approaches the mouth while the child leans back. This altered situation again produces a changed visual stimulation as the hand approaches the mouth, as well as further kinesthetic changes. This new visual, kinesthetic, and tactual stimulation discriminatively guides muscle actions which bring the hand to the lips, producing a new tactual stimulation from pea and fingertips against the lips, and losing much of the previous visual stimulation as the child's hand moves largely out of sight under his nose. This new pattern occasions insertion of the pea into the mouth, which cues tongue and jaw responses to chew and swallow the pea (the already well-organized respondent chain, peristalsis). The chain is then complete, from the point of view of discriminating differentiated arm and hand movements. (From the biological point of view, the process continues as processes of digestion, assimilation, and metabolism.)

In these examples the chain of responses ends in the accurate placing of some object in the mouth. The fact that the infant's world contains food objects that are reinforcing to place in the mouth is a great ally to these chains of motor development. But if we recall the probability that sucking-produced stimuli become positive acquired reinforcers early in development (Chapter 6) and examine hand-to-mouth behavior in the young infant we realize that part of the behavior chains are already established before the sequences described here take place.

The young infant lying prone or supine on his bed is in a position conducive to flexion of both arms toward the head. As a result the infant's hands are usually within a few inches of his mouth. A slight flexion of the arm may bring the hand into contact with the lips. A small amount of trial and error will get the hand or thumb into the mouth; and if it is reinforcing to the infant to suck on such objects, then this chain of further flexing the arm and inserting the thumb into the mouth is correspondingly strengthened. Since the chain is both a short and a probable one (due to the infant's characteristic position), differentiation of the behavior into successively more accurate performances should go on steadily, and a gradual extension of the early part of the chain naturally will be seen. That is, the infant learns to bring his hand accurately to his mouth from successively greater distances and, gradually, from a greater variety of positions of the arm.

As a result, when the infant later confronts a pea or an egg on his table top, the greatest contribution of that environment to his motor development will be in the chains of reaching accurately for the object; he will already be skillful in bringing the captured pea or egg directly to his mouth.

Obviously, the infant's world is filled with similar situations which result in similar learnings. The result of a wealth of such experiences is an infant who can accurately reach for and finely manipulate a great variety of objects that he sees, feels, hears, smells, etc. Given such a backlog of learning, the discrimination of differentiated finger responses to a specific visual and kinesthetic stimulus is primarily a matter of refining already learned differentiations, and in this sense the infant's environment teaches him all adult manual dexterity.

The development of complex motor skills takes place slowly in typical infant development. To some extent, the shaping of response patterns may be attributed to the fact that the infant encounters instructing environments by chance and in random fashion. Much everyday experience that could be instructive is not effective at the moment it occurs, because more basic skills have not yet been formed. The pea, for example, provides an excellent situation for the teaching of finger skills. But for the child who cannot yet accurately place even a hand on an object as small as a pea, this opportunity for finger shaping is necessarily lost to him. And for the infant who cannot yet sit up in a baby table, even the opportunity to learn to place a hand accurately on a table top must wait.

Skills sometimes must be learned in sequences, the more basic ones being prerequisite for the more advanced. As a result, many of the developing motor chains of infants will appear in quite standard sequences, and have often been described as if they represented a natural sequence of some physiological process, mostly neural maturation. However, they may represent a natural sequence of prerequisites in motor chains as described above. Halverson gives a detailed example of the sequential development of prehension (Gesell, 1954 and Halverson, 1931). At about 20 weeks of age, the average infant shows an infirm touching and squeezing responses; by 28 weeks he closes the palm but not the fingers about an object; by 36 weeks the forefinger is used differentially to finger objects as well as palm them; by 60 weeks, all of the finger movements have become somewhat differentiated, as well as the thumb, and the child's grasp much resembles that of an adult in the separate or combined use of fingers, thumb, and palm. It seems clear that each of these behaviors may well be necessary to shaping of the next simply as a matter of sequencing, rather than as a process of maturing.

Since a great deal of the child's experiences in the development of skills are happenstance, it would be difficult to estimate what the fastest pace of such learning would be. Students of infant motor development have assumed that a slow pace is inherent in the neural constitution of the infant: "Training in any particular activity before the neural mechanisms have reached a certain stage of readiness is futile" (McGraw, 1943).

Unfortunately, the direct study of the neural development of the infant in relationship to the complexity of behavior he can be taught at each stage of that development is equally untried. It is known that certain neural fibers are not as completely covered at birth with a fatty substance, myelin, as they will be in a few more months; and it is thought that this substance acts as a sort of insulator for the nervous fiber, preventing signals from being diffused or lost into adjoining tissue. But it is not known how *much* myelinization is necessary for a given degree of motor coordination in an infant. It would seem that the method for establishing the limits of learning for an infant at a given age would be to teach him skills in as effective and skillful a manner as could be accomplished. Success in such a venture would always be informative; but failure might mean only that the techniques used to shape the infant's behavior were not as effective as they could have been, and would thereby call for another attempt, hopefully a better one. In short, the proper study of the limits of learning is the constant attempt to achieve learning beyond what is currently presumed to be the limits.

BODY MANAGEMENT AND LOCOMOTION

Our discussion thus far has been specific to the development of finger, hand, and arm dexterity. The principles exemplified in this analysis, however, are general. They apply to the development of neck, tongue, eye, trunk, leg, and foot skills, and to those involving the use of the entire body. We can observe a multitude of environments which operate to shape such behaviors. Any environment may be analyzed to see what body movements are followed by reinforcing consequences.

For example, an infant lying on a toy with hard, sharp corners is continuously stimulated by a negative reinforcer, escape from which will strengthen any response chain producing that escape. This situation is one in which a complex of kinesthetic and tactual stimuli, depending on the position of the child's limbs and his position in his crib, can become a discriminative stimulus for a chain of arm, leg, and trunk responses which roll the child over and off the offending toy. Lying on his stomach over the object will be discriminative for one sort of the chain, lying on his back over the object will be discriminative for another, lying on his side on the object for still another, and so on.

As another example, consider an infant seated in a stroller; if the stroller is turned so that the child faces directly into strong sunlight, he is being exposed to a negative reinforcer. (As shown in Chapters 3 and 6, almost any kind of stimulus, if present in sufficient intensity, will function as a negative reinforcer.) Intense sun on the face constitutes an environment which can teach the infant a number of response chains involving his neck muscles involved in turning of the head and reduction in intensity of the light on the eyes. Responses with the eyes and eyelids which accomplish the same partial withdrawal of the negative reinforcer will also increase in strength. All of these chains will be discriminated to stimuli associated with the direction of the strong light on the basis of the kinds of head movements which will remove the stimulus and the kinds which will not remove the stimulus.

The blanket, as a reinforcer, contributes to the infant's developing motor coordination, since it reinforces chains ot responses which rearrange it. The reinforcing stimulation at the end of these chains could be the feel, sight, nearness, or the holding of the blanket. The blanket may also reinforce behaviors of carrying it about as the infant becomes a toddler, which can contribute to developing his balancing skills. The sight of the baby toting his blanket may entertain the parents and other onlookers, producing social stimuli such as attention and laughter, which may also serve as reinforcers. If so, the behavior of carrying the blanket can be further strengthened, persisting as long as it functions as an attention-getter. The social reinforcement of behavior in relation to the blanket would add still further to the generalized status of the blanket as a discriminative stimulus: it is then a discriminative stimulus for social as well as for physical reinforcers.

The ordinary experiences of an infant include frequent interactions with *moderate* intensities of various negative reinforcers. Consequently, chains which avoid and escape from these stimuli can develop early in life, contributing to the steadily increasing efficiency and skill of the infant in the use of his body. In the same way, clumsy responses will be weakened, as they present negative reinforcers. Such ineffective interactions with things contribute to body management and locomotor skills in a negative way.

If rest and sleep are reinforcing for infants, then responses leading to rest and sleep would be strengthened in such circumstances. Many and various skills of body arrangement which make for the most relaxed position and thereby the easiest transition from wakefulness to sleep thus will develop.

As we have pointed out previously in this chapter, simply the possession of a thumb constitutes an environment which may prove instructive for the young infant. Let us elaborate: if the stimuli produced by the infant's thumbsucking are reinforcing (and there is excellent reason to expect that this stimulation will become reinforcing, if it is not initially), then the infant is always in a position to strengthen any chains of arm responses which bring the thumb to his mouth. We have already pointed out the likelihood that the shortest and simplest of chains would be established early in the infant's development. Consider now some of the longer and more complicated chains that may be shaped subsequently. Most of these would be controlled most effectively by the kinesthetic stimuli provided by the position of the infant's arm in the various positions it may take and in the course of movement which brings the thumb to the mouth. In some situations, the infant's arm may be restrained by clothes, blankets, or the position of his own body (as when he lies on his arm). Thus, more complex chains may be developed. The initial part of these chains often will involve manipulating the clothes, blankets, or the rest of his own body, so as to free the arm; the subsequent part of these chains then would be the already familiar one of bringing the thumb to the mouth once the arm is free. In this way, more complex and lengthy chains of response, including a steadily growing variety of skills, are formed. Most of the physical environments which accomplish instruction in basic body skills will have this characteristic of subsequently shaping ever longer and more complex chains of increasingly coordinated behaviors.

REFERENCES

Curti, M. W. *Child psychology.* New York: Longmans, Green, 1930.

Gesell, A. The ontogenesis of infant behavior. In L. Carmichael (Ed.) *Manual of child psychology.* (2nd ed.) New York: Wiley, 1954.

Halverson, H. M. An experimental study of prehension in infants by means of systematic cinema records. *Genet. Psychol. Monogr.*, 1931, *10*, 107–286.

Hurlock, Elizabeth B. *Child development.* (4th ed.) New York: McGraw-Hill, 1964, pp. 111–207.

McGraw, Myrtle B. *The neuromuscular maturation of the human infant.* New York: Columbia Univer. Press, 1943.

Munn, N. L. *The evolution and growth of human behavior.* Boston: Houghton Mifflin, 1951, pp. 276–302.

Thompson, G. G. *Child development.* (2nd ed.) Boston: Houghton Mifflin, 1962, pp. 223–270.

Socialization — The Development of Behavior to Social Stimuli

The skill of an infant in manipulating his physical world with reinforcing consequences is a steadily but slowly developing one. Consequently, in the early stages of development, the reinforcers necessary for life must be arranged for him by the person who performs the usual mothering functions—feeding, bathing, changing, and the like. In doing so, she also provides social stimuli (see Vol. I, p. 17, for a classification of stimuli). The principles describing the development of behavior to these social stimuli are not different from those describing his development to physical and organismic stimuli. However, social stimuli are distinctive enough to merit separate discussion, as are the consequences of this development for the infant's future behavior (Gewirtz, 1961).

DEVELOPMENT OF THE DISCRIMINATIVE FUNCTION OF MOTHER FOR REINFORCING EVENTS

A newborn baby is a thoroughly helpless creature. Without consistent care, he certainly will not survive. All of the frequent and consistent care he requires must be provided by others. In our culture (as in many) it is usually the mother who does most of this; the father does some, too, and other relatives, like grandparents and older siblings, may take a hand. We shall refer to the person providing the care as the "mother," whoever the person may be on any specific occasion.

The essential function of the mother is to provide positive reinforcers to the infant and remove negative ones. This is not the ordinary description a mother gives of her duties, but it is a technical one—a functional and fairly comprehensive specification of her behavior as a mother. Thus, she feeds her infant six to eight times a day at first, frequently ensures that his skin temperature is neither too hot nor too cold, holds him to her and strokes him, rescues him from any situation which she thinks is hurting him, adds toys to his crib, moves him and the objects in his world about, and puts him to bed for rest and sleep.

In doing these things and many others, the mother herself will, as a stimulus object, become discriminated as a "time" and a place for either the addition of positive reinforcers to the baby's environment or the subtraction of negative reinforcers from it. Thus she is discriminative, as a stimulus, for the two reinforcement procedures which strengthen operant behavior. Thereby, she acquires positive reinforcing function, and lays the foundation for the further social development of her infant.

The mother is discriminative for some reinforcement procedures by necessity, and for others by accident or through common cultural practice. To illustrate this, we consider a number of reinforcers separately, noting the discriminative role of the mother for each.

Food and Water

The mother feeds the infant several times a day, every day for many months. If she is breast-feeding the child, then she is a stimulus that appears just before the receipt of milk (and sucking stimulation, too) and one that remains throughout the nursing period. If she is bottle-feeding him, she accompanies the initial presentation of the bottle, and the insertion of the nipple into the infant's mouth. Typically, she holds both infant and bottle throughout the feeding, thus remaining discriminative for milk throughout the ingestion process. Occasionally, she may prop up infant and bottle and leave for a time; even so, she has been discriminative for the first milk's presentation.

Even as the infant develops increasing competence to feed himself, the mother still retains much of her discriminative function for reinforcement derived from feeding. She typically prepares the food and places it before the infant or hands it to him. Indeed, long into his later life, when he is capable of preparing for himself, she continues to engage in the cultural practice of feeding him.

Taste Stimuli

The nearly universal behavior of giving candy to children may be singled out (somewhat arbitrarily) from the other feeding behaviors of the mother. Candy certainly is a food, but it often is given to children when they are fairly satiated with other foods, and presumably is consumed primarily for its taste. Cookies and fruit juices are also instances of distinctive tastes given to children by mothers. Thus the mother is discriminative for taste reinforcement too. However, the infant encounters some tastes without the help of the mother, since he sucks on nearly every object which can be fitted into his mouth. Some of these objects will have a taste that may be reinforcing. Some of these will be positive reinforcers, but some will be negative. Tastes of objects given by the mother, however, are almost always positive ones (except when she must give the child evil-tasting medicines).

Skin Temperature

The infant's internal temperature is self-regulating. His skin temperature, however, depends on the temperature of his surroundings and the kinds and numbers of layers of clothing and blankets covering his body. For the regulation of external temperature change, he must at first depend upon his mother. By removing layers of clothing when he is hot, and adding them when he is cold, she marks an occasion of removal of a negative reinforcer and return of a positive one. Later, as part of the baby's increase in motor skills, he learns to dress and undress himself and adjust his own blankets, whereupon the mother loses much of her discriminative function from this source. Until then, however, her role is definitely discriminative.

Rest and Sleep

The very young infant typically rests and sleeps most of his day. Many infants can drop off to sleep anywhere and anytime, and the sight of an infant sleeping in a grocery cart, stroller, car seat, on a store counter, or in the aisle is not uncommon. Thus no help from the mother is consistently needed to mark occasions of rest and sleep reinforcement. However, cultural practices may give the mother a role in the infant's rest and sleep routines that would make her discriminative for rest and sleep. It is common in our society for a baby (or older child) to be "put to bed." This practice may consist of a change of clothes (usually into sleeping garments), placing the child in his crib, covering him with blankets, and sometimes, singing a lullaby; alternatively, it may consist of rocking and perhaps singing until the baby is asleep or shows signs of drowsiness. Through this feature of child-rearing practice the mother gratuitously acquires a discriminative function for rest and sleep reinforcers.

Tactual Stimulation

It is a common practice in our society for mothers to hold their infants. For one thing, this is often the only way to transport them; moreover, it sometimes quiets them and, thirdly, it is often reinforcing to the mother. Another common practice of mothers in our society is to pet and stroke their infants, to kiss them, to tap them on the "tummy," and to ruffle their hair (however sparse). These customs, too, seem to provide some reinforcement for the mother, possibly because of the tactual stimulation provided by the baby and his responses to such stimulation. At any rate, such practices provide tactual stimulation to the baby. If this type of tactual stimulation is reinforcing, and it seems to be in most instances, then the mother is discriminative for it. However, it is a discriminative function she shares with a variety of other stimuli, such as the baby's blanket, his clothes, his Teddy Bear, the cat, etc. In other words, the mother may be a significant source of tactual reinforcement, but she is by no means the only source, especially as the baby grows older.

Opportunity to Breathe

The infant does his own breathing, of course. On infrequent occasions (see Chapter 6), breathing may prove difficult for him, as when he has croup or asthma, or has managed to get his nose and mouth thoroughly covered by something he cannot remove by his own actions. On the occasions of internal obstructions brought about by physiological disturbances, mother may rescue him, perhaps by taking him into a warm, moist place (the bathroom with a hot shower running, seems a favorite prescription); or possibly by holding him upright, a position in which congested respiratory passages drain better. When breathing has been obstructed accidentally by such things as pillows or clinging sheets of plastic, it is necessary for the mother to remove them since the baby cannot. Thus there are scattered times when the mother takes on a discriminative role for the opportunity for the infant to breathe better. These occurrences are quite rare, but when they do occur they may be urgent (highly aversive) from the infant's point of view. Thus it is worthwhile to note these kinds of contributions to the mother's discriminative role.

Negative Reinforcers

Despite meticulous care, negative reinforcers manage to act upon the infant from time to time. He may, for example, roll upon hard toys, pinch himself between mattress and crib bars, bang his head into the headboard, be exposed to hot, bright sunlight, have gastric pains, cut a tooth, and be manhandled by an older sibling or a house pet. From some of these accidents, the mother must rescue him, thereby functioning as a stimulus discriminative for the removal of negative reinforcers. She can, for example, roll him off the hard object, free him from the clutches of the mattress and crib, move him into the shade, "burp" him, massage his gums, and drive off the older sibling or pet.

In many situations she can do little about removing negative reinforcers, since they have had their full impact before she can get into effective action. Yet even in these instances, she often plays something of a discriminative role by virtue of the nature of the course of a hurt. When an infant experiences a negative reinforcer, he usually cries. This respondent signal of distress often attracts the mother, who, seeing that he has been hurt but that it is all over, nevertheless picks him up and comforts him. In so doing, she marks an occasion of the waning of the stimulus which hurt him. Speaking loosely, he is just starting to feel better and there he is in mother's arms. How is he to know it wasn't mother who actually reduced the intensity of the hurt?

Stimulus Change

If stimulus change is reinforcing to an infant, then at least some stimulus change is provided by the mother. She picks him up and moves him from one place to another, she places new toys in his view; she speaks and sings to him; and she plays games with him, such as peek-a-boo, patty-cake, and making faces. Thus, her appearance on the scene frequently is discriminative for rather widespread stimulus changes. Indeed, the younger the infant, the less accomplished he is in arranging his environment to produce changes; hence long hours in his crib constitute a considerable deprivation of stimulus change, and the greater is his dependence upon the mother to make something happen. As the baby grows older, however, many more responses which produce such changes become available to him, and hence the mother will constitute a smaller source of stimulus change in his total environment. Thus mother's initial discriminative status for much of this kind of reinforcement will diminish during the course of development.

Control of Environment

If it is reinforcing to an infant to control his environment as described in Chapter 6, then it should be true that in the early days of development this control is highly imperfect. In such instances, an ally could provide the aid necessary to turn failure into success. The mother often is such an ally, helping the baby to pick up and hold objects, pushing things so that they are within his reach, propping up objects so that they will stand, etc. In so doing, she is discriminative for the baby's exercising greater control of his environment than he could effect in her absence. To the extent that this happens, it adds to the discriminative status of the mother.

DEVELOPMENT OF THE DISCRIMINATIVE FUNCTIONS OF MOTHER FOR AVERSIVE EVENTS

The preceding discussion has concentrated on the actions of the mother which make her discriminative for the addition of positive reinforcers and the removal of negative ones. Obviously, there will be occasions when she will have the reverse discriminative role: she will take away positive reinforcers and add negative reinforcers. For example, she may remove tasty substances from the baby's mouth on the grounds that they are not edible; she may take away entertaining objects because they are sharp or economically valuable; or she may wake up the baby because she must give him medicine or take him with her on an errand. Through clumsiness, she may occasionally bump or drop the baby; she may deliver him to doctors who must stick him with needles; she may force nasty-tasting medicines upon him; or she may scrub him with more vigor than is necessary. In all of these examples and many similar ones, the mother develops and adds to her acquired negative reinforcing function, not her acquired positive reinforcing function.

In Volume I, we referred to the operation or act of taking away positive reinforcers and adding negative reinforcers as "punishment by loss" and "punishment by hurt" (p. 37). These terms, borrowed from everyday language, are only loose descriptions of the interactions involved. It would be more accurate to say that under the circumstances described the mother develops a discriminative function for aversive stimulation. (This phrase also carries fewer unintended meanings.) The mere presence of the mother during these acts of aversive stimulation makes it likely that some stimulus aspect of her behavior will develop conditioned aversive functions. If it can be demonstrated that the behavior which accomplishes the removal of that aspect of mother is strengthened, then we may say that she has acquired negative reinforcing functions.

In general, of course, aversive occurrences are far fewer than those in which the mother adds positive and subtracts negative reinforcers. In balancing the two sets of circumstances, then, the acquired reinforcing function of the mother is usually positive. How strongly positive she is depends upon the proportion of times she is discriminative for the addition of positive and the subtraction of negative reinforcers relative to the proportion of the subtraction of positive and the addition of negative reinforcers. Her overall reinforcement strength also depends on the value of the positive and negative reinforcers involved, the baby's relevant deprivation states, the schedules of reinforcement involved, and so on. Thus, depending upon how the mother performs her functions, her net strength as an acquired positive reinforcer is determined.

It is conceivable that the mother could be more discriminative for the removal of positive reinforcers and the presentation of negative ones than the opposite. In that case, her overall acquired reinforcing function would be negative. This is certainly possible with older children. In the case of infants, however, it may well be that the actual survival of the infant requires that the mother has been discriminative for the presentation of positive reinforcers and the removal of negative ones more often and more intensively than for the removal of positive reinforcers and the addition of negative ones, at least during the first year or so. Thus, for all infants who survive their first months of development, we may assume that their mothers have acquired at least some reinforcing function.

THE STIMULUS COMPONENTS OF THE MOTHER

The functional characterization of the mother presented thus far is that of a discriminative social stimulus. Having outlined what she is discriminative for, it is now appropriate to identify more precisely the stimuli involved.

The equation of a person to a stimulus is of course an oversimplification. There are innumerable ways of characterizing the stimuli which make up a human being. Many of these, however, will have little or no functional value for the behavior of other people, especially of their children. For example, we might describe a mother by the number of calories of heat she radiated per hour. This is certainly one of her stimulus characteristics, but it is of little significance to her baby unless the mother provides a source of heat for the baby in an otherwise cold environment. Similarly, a mother could be characterized by the number of hairs on her head. Her baby may respond to the color of her hair and the shape of its arrangement on her head, but he is not responsive to the number of discrete hairs.

The characteristics of a mother which are important stimuli for her baby clearly are those which are involved in her discriminative functions. In effect, they are the stimuli, in all their variety, which allow the mother to be discriminated from the rest of the house and the objects in it and from other people who are not caretakers, at least to some degree. To a great extent, these are visual stimuli; but auditory, tactual, and olfactory stimulus elements also play a part. The mother has the usual shape of *homo sapiens* plus her own individual biological differences. The shape is seen by the baby in a variety of wrappings and positions, some more often than others.

The baby's initial discriminations may be no more elegant than that reinforcement often follows the appearance of a certain shape wrapped in gray bending over him. The shape has a distinctive top, a face crowned with hair. The hair is of fairly constant color (ordinarily), but is seen in a variety of arrangements about the face. The face has certain constant elements consisting of its basic lines, the shape of the nose, and so on. The variations on the patterns of the face are considerable, however, ranging from broad smiles to stormy frowns. Some of these arrangements, such as smiles, may be more discriminative for positive reinforcement than others, such as frowns. The shape has a voice which occasionally makes noise, and the frequencies and tenor of this noise are fairly consistent. It does, however, include coos, gurgles, shouts, and happy, angry, and placid tones. The happy sounds may be more reliable cues for positive reinforcers than the angry ones (which, in time, often will be clearly discriminative for negative reinforcers). The specific patterns of sound making up the mother's language will initially have little discriminative value for the infant. Later they will acquire this function, and after about five years of age these sounds will control a highly complex assortment of discriminated operants.

The mother also has a number of surfaces providing tactual stimulation which the infant might experience. These stimuli are provided by her skin (especially her hands), the clothes she wears, and her hair. The touch of the mother's hands may be discriminative for subsequent reinforcement. The feel of the mother's face sometimes might be modified by a layer of cosmetics or of perspiration. The feel of her clothes obviously will be a frequently changeable stimulus.

The mother also might provide a number of odors. Some of these are eminently associated with her appearance; some are added from time to time by perfumes, cosmetics, mouthwashes and toothpastes, smoking, and the like. It is unlikely that any of the latter are particularly discriminative for any reinforcing consequences for the infant (except, possibly, that a highly perfumed and made-up mother is likely to leave soon and be replaced by another person [babysitter]. The nature of this sequence of events is hardly systematic in its effects. It depends upon the types of care given by the mother and the substitute mother).

These are at least some of the stimuli, then, which contribute to the baby's recognition of the mother. They allow him to discriminate her from other parts of his environment which also have shapes, make sounds, and provide tactual and olfactory stimulation. But because so many stimuli from mother vary within wide limits, it is necessary to consider her not as a fixed class of stimuli, but rather as a continuously changing array of stimuli from many classes. The classes of stimuli from which the mother's samples of stimuli are drawn are, of course, shared by other people. Thus the positions of the mother's body relative to the baby are duplicated by many other bodies from time to time, and clothes on the mother are much like those of others who come and go. Perhaps no one else has quite the mother's nose, but the general shape and location of her nose relative to her eyes and mouth, and the variations of facial contours arranged by smiles, frowns, and the like, are like the facial expressions of others. The mother's voice may have a characteristic tenor and style of inflection, but the voices of many persons produce similar frequencies and inflections, and share much of the same language, idioms, and exclamations. Other individuals will feel much like the mother to the baby and, on occasion, will also provide similar odors.

In effect, the mother is a changing sample of stimuli, some of which are unique to her, but many of which are shared by other people. Thus stimuli from a mother which become discriminative for reinforcement may overlap with stimuli from other people, and the baby's behaviors which have become strengthened to mother's stimulation may be evoked by others who present the same or similar stimuli. Consequently, there are natural bases for both *discrimination* of the mother from all other people and for *generalization* from the mother to others. Thus, the baby can unfailingly pick out his parents when necessary; yet, just as he smiles at them, makes noises, waves, claps, and does other "tricks" for them, so he may do the same for others, even without previous direct experience with them.

As the mother becomes a social reinforcer for the baby, other people acquire a generalized reinforcing value (to the extent that they, as samples of stimuli, are like the mother). This process may be the basic learning operation which gives the child a social character and allows the figurative label of man as a "social animal." That is, man is an organism whose mother, in being discriminative for reinforcement, is sufficiently changeable as a stimulus complex to be much like other people he meets later in his life; he will respond to them at least in part as he has responded to his mother. (It is often said that the child learns about society "through the eyes of his mother.") Basically, the mother has been discriminative for the presentation of positive and for the removal of negative reinforcers; therefore the child's mother, and, by generalization, others similar to her, will acquire the stimulus property of a positive acquired reinforcer, i.e., a social reinforcer.

It is now essential to analyze in more specific terms the stimuli of the mother which are discriminative for behaviors leading to reinforcement. So far, discussion has centered on stimuli which make it apparent that the mother is distinct from other parts of the baby's environment. But the mother provides cues which are a part of the reinforcement procedures she performs; she provides more detailed stimuli: her *proximity* or nearness, her *attention*, and her *affection* or warmth. These stimulus components of the mother are of special significance for the future development of the baby and child.

Proximity of the Mother to the Baby

The majority of reinforcement operations the mother performs are administered in close physical relationship to the baby. Mother cannot feed the baby, adjust his temperature, rescue him from hurtful objects, hold him, or prepare him for sleep at a distance. Such caretaking functions require handling of the baby while providing reinforcers, and thus the mother, to reinforce, must be near the baby—within reaching distance, at least. As a consequence, mother at a distance is hardly discriminative for reinforcement, but mother nearby is discriminative.

The stimulus dimensions involved in reacting to objects at different distances away, or distance perception, have long been an interesting problem in visual perception and discrimination. For an adult, the cues reacted to in discriminating distance include at least: (1) the angle of convergence the eyeballs assume in fixating an object at various distances, (2) the disparity or differences in images falling on the two retinas, (3) the texture, brightness, and parallel line characteristics, and (4) the interposition of other objects between the viewer and the object (Gibson, 1950). An infant may not use all of these cues in discriminating distances; indeed, some of them may be learned during his early days in the child-rearing situations under discussion. In these situations, the mother in close proximity to the baby is more discriminative for reinforcement than the mother at a distance, and it follows that any stimuli marking these differences in distance will themselves become functional for the baby. If mother is close, reinforcement follows, sometimes after a short delay; if mother is far, reinforcement follows only after a long delay or not at all.

The nearness of the mother is one of the basic social discriminative stimuli. Closeness-to-the-mother thereby takes on positive reinforcing power, and behaviors of the baby producing proximity of the mother will be strengthened, while behaviors losing this proximity will be weakened. For the young baby who does not move about, certain responses often will produce the essential proximity of a mother. These include crying and fussing, calling "Mommy," or any responses with objects that make noise of the sort that will attract a curious parent. Certain facial expressions of a "cute" sort often will attract a distant adult, as may other tricks which mothers interpret as especially charming or advanced, such as playing patty-cake.

For the baby who moves about, creeping, crawling, toddling, walking, or running are some of the responses that can produce the proximity of the mother and maintain it as the mother moves about. Tagging along after the mother is clearly one of the most prominent behaviors of young children, and may be viewed as a set of discriminated operants maintained by the proximity functioning as a positive reinforcer. The contribution of this basic social reinforcer to increasing skill and speed in locomotor behaviors may be great; it has often been clinically described (frequently in terms of the baby's need for security) but has not as yet been experimentally analyzed. However, Gewirtz (1954) has made an analysis of the role of proximity in stimulating a number of social responses such as attention-seeking.

Proximity should be a less distinctive stimulus for babies reared in small living quarters than for those living in large houses. Where the environment is quite small, as in a cramped one-room apartment, the mother is rarely far from the baby. Thus the difference between a distant mother and a near one is minimal: the mother when she is giving reinforcers is hardly much nearer than when she is not. When the baby and mother live in a large room, however, the nonreinforcing mother may be much farther away than when she is reinforcing, and the distance dimension is much more prominent. In a house with many rooms, the nonreinforcing mother may frequently be out of the child's sight, and the role of proximity as a distinctive cue for reinforcement is maximized.

Casual observation shows that many young crawlers and toddlers spend a considerable proportion of their waking day near the mother. Even when a special room has been equipped with attractive toys for the baby, the mother may find that these play objects are displaced to the vicinity of her feet as she stands washing dishes at the kitchen sink and that, in effect, her baby's recreation room is whatever room she is in at the time. Although proximity seems to be a rather simple pattern of stimuli, it is a potent social reinforcer for babies and young children.

Proximity may not remain potent. It may even reverse its function from being discriminative for positive stimulation to being discriminative for aversive stimulation under special circumstances. If, for example, a mother should become very punitive, giving more negative than positive reinforcers, her proximity becomes a discriminative stimulus for aversive stimulation or punishment. Proximity thereby acquires a negative reinforcing function which may override and displace its previously acquired positive function. The child may avoid her nearness. To put it simply, he cannot be spanked from a distance.

Paying Attention to the Baby

Just as the mother must be near in order to reinforce, she must also be attentive to present positive and remove negative reinforcers with any degree of effectiveness. It is difficult to imagine her feeding her baby, adjusting his clothes or blankets, or rescuing him from harm without paying some attention to him in the process. Her attention is another aspect of her behavior which, as a social stimulus, is discriminative for reinforcement for her baby. Like her proximity, her attention is a constellation of stimuli which will become increasingly established as a social reinforcer for her baby.

The physical components of attention are complex. One of the prominent features of attentive behavior involves *looking at the object or person* attended to. The attentive mother will often be a person whose face is pointed at the baby, the eyes aimed directly at him in a distance angle of convergence. Frequently, the mother's entire body will *turn toward the baby*, if she was oriented elsewhere just previously. This motion, too, will be a part of the act of attending. There may be characteristic *vocal stimuli*, such as "Hi, baby" or "What's wrong, baby?" *Facial changes* include the raising of eyebrows in the fashion characteristic of adult interrogation. If the mother had previously been occupied with something else, there may be a sudden *cessation of other activity* as her attention is captured by the baby. These and similar stimuli are generated by the responses mother makes as she attends on various reinforcement occasions.

The stimuli she displays in paying attention are discriminative for the reinforcement procedures she practices, and will become discriminated by her baby. The variability in style of attending by various mothers will correspond to the various kinds of attention which will prove reinforcing to their children later in life. Thus some children may be more reinforced by a quiet audience and others may be more reinforced by highly talkative company. The differences in the kind of effective reinforcer may be due to mothers who attended quietly with the former group and noisily with the latter.

It should be pointed out that these differences may also be due to a more recent reinforcement history. For example, a baby may have had a quiet mother and thus be more reinforced by quiet attention than by noisy. However, later in school, he may find that when the teacher talks or reads to him, it is generally a positive state of affairs, but that when he talks (recites) to the quietly attentive teacher, he often receives correction and disapproval (and perhaps ridicule from unsympathetic classmates). These school experiences might well reverse his previous rank order of responsiveness to these two forms of attention.

In babies and young children the behaviors which are strengthened by attention are similar to those strengthened by proximity of a positive social reinforcer. Any behaviors on the part of the baby which are delightful, *or* irritating, or otherwise significant to the mother will attract her attention, and the behaviors involved in her paying attention to the baby are strengthened. Note that some of the baby's most effective behaviors in getting the mother's attention are crying, fussing, and fretting. These responses produce stimuli which constitute negative reinforcers to the mother. The mother, in an effort to terminate this type of behavior (and thereby escape from the negative reinforcers these sights and sounds constitute), will attend to the baby, seeking the stimulus or condition responsible for it. To the extent that such fussing involves operant behaviors (and this could be considerable), these behaviors are strengthened by her attention.

Situations involving slight frustrations for the baby (which initially elicit crying as a respondent process) become thus discriminative for the operant responses as a part of crying and fussing, since on such occasions these operants are frequently reinforced with the mother's attending behaviors. One possible result: fussing, as a discriminated operant, becomes a prevalent form of behavior of the baby. This type of outcome is distasteful to most mothers, yet it occurs frequently, for the mother becomes involved in a detrimental contingency. Since the baby's crying is a negative reinforcer for her, she attends to the baby and is immediately reinforced by the stopping of the crying. By so doing, she makes it more likely that *operant crying* will occur again on the next occasion of slight frustration for the baby. As *operant* crying grows in strength, the range of occasions on which it occurs increases correspondingly. If it is reinforced with mother's attention in these new situations, too, then it becomes generalized further to a greater variety of situations, and a disadvantageous cycle results, the outcome being a baby who cries in almost any situation.

For the mother, this situation may be a distressing state of affairs, yet she will in all probability continue to attend to such annoying behaviors, since she is reinforced for doing so by the temporary cessations of the baby's fussing behaviors. Simple extinction of crying (not attending) may serve to disrupt the cycle. Note, however, that the mother's behavior of attending to fussing must be inhibited at the same time. Note, too, that it would be desirable for the mother to be alert to reinforce at the same time the kinds of behaviors she would prefer to strengthen, such as asking or calling. Note, finally, that it would be highly inappropriate and even detrimental for the mother to cease attending to all of her baby's crying, since on some occasions it would represent responses (respondents) to genuinely harmful circumstances (aversive) from which she must rescue her baby.

This example illustrates a critical characteristic of mother's behavior in giving attention to her children. "Bad" behavior is consistently attended to, in many instances more consistently than "good" behavior. To the extent that her attention functions as a positive reinforcer, any behaviors on the part of the baby, bad as well as good, that produce attention will be strengthened. If bad behaviors are more consistently attended to, they may well strengthen faster than the good ones. This simple formula suggests that a child's behavior may become increasingly and systematically more distasteful to his mother. That this frequently does *not* happen suggests the operation of other processes in addition to the one described here. However, that this frequently *does* happen suggests that the principle is a powerful one, and sometimes does operate more consistently than others which would produce a happier outcome. (A fuller discussion of this principle is reserved for Volume III, which deals with older children of greater competence in both bad and good behaviors.)

Affection Toward the Baby

Some mothers are prompted to display affection by the reinforcing occasions involved in child rearing practices. On such occasions their affection takes the form of smiles, kisses, hugs, and pats, special crooning tones of voice, loving words, nuzzling, hair-ruffling, tickling, and similar behaviors associated with delighted and effusive parents. Other mothers are, by contrast, inclined to provide affection most reliably only when they are in the midst of an affectionate display generated by conditions not directly associated with child caring activities. In either situation there is a correlation between such stimuli and reinforcement which is sufficient to give the affectionate stimuli discriminative status. As with attention, the variability in individual mothers' styles of being affectionate will correspond to the kinds of affection which will prove maximally reinforcing for their children later. Thus, some children may be more responsive to smiles than to extravagant displays of hugging, kissing, and fondling; others may be more reinforced by an affectionate word or phrase; still others may be most susceptible to a pat on the head, and so on.

Few experimental studies have been conducted to provide specific information on affectionate stimuli, the range of their physical properties, the probable time of their initial effectiveness, etc. One study by Brackbill on smiling (1958) is described because it is instructive for further research in this area.

Brackbill's study of smiling in four-month-old infants was generated by her interest in the response in relation to its presumed social nature and its early role in social learning. The infants chosen were old enough to remain awake throughout the experimental sessions, young enough not to respond discriminatively to "mother" versus "others," placid enough not to cry too often during sessions and to lie on their backs for at least five minutes without struggling, and responsive enough to show an operant level of at least two smiles within a five-minute session. Brackbill does not give a verbal description of smiling, but reports that prior to the main study, she and another judge observed some 970 occasions of smiling or nonsmiling in infants, and agreed in 97.5% of their judgments.

Two limiting factors should be kept in mind in reviewing this study. First, smiling (like vocalization) is a lingering response in infants, which adds to the difficulty in perceiving changes in its rate. Second, limitations were imposed by the length of time it took to offer the social reinforcement given as a consequence of smiling: "Five seconds were required for picking S up; 30 seconds for reinforcement; five seconds for putting S down; and five seconds for recording. Therefore, no more than six responses could occur and be reinforced during any five-minute interval" (p. 117).

Despite these less than ideal conditions, the experimental conditions, which consisted of (1) an operant level period, (2) a conditioning period (of either continuous or intermittent reinforcement), and (3) an extinction period, produced differences in smiling frequencies. The operant level was taken as the rate observed through at least eight separate five-minute intervals, during which the investigator stood motionless over the infant (who lay on his back in his crib), and maintained an expressionless face at about 15 inches from the infant's face. During conditioning sessions (consisting of 10 to 12 five-minute intervals), the investigator reinforced smiling by smiling at, picking up, and cuddling the infant, using continuous reinforcement with one group and working steadily from continuous to variable ratios of 1, 2, 3, and 4 with another group. (These behaviors typify the activities of many affectionate mothers.) Extinction was similar to the operant level condition, and was observed over 15 or more five-minute intervals.

The rate of smiling during the conditioning period was reliably higher than the rate during the operant level. During extinction, the intermittently reinforced group extinguished less rapidly; both groups fell below their previous operant level rate of smiling, and both displayed "protest" behavior to the unsmiling investigator, crying or turning away from her.

All subjects were studied immediately after nursing and following a nap. The mother in each case phoned Brackbill when her infant awoke, and Brackbill arrived at the infant's home to work with a freshly diapered infant just satiated with food. The mother cooperated to the extent of engaging in minimal contact with the infant prior to each experimental session. The study took place in the infant's own home and crib.

Returning to the general concept of affection, it seems that affection is a much more variable stimulus constellation than is either proximity or attention. It is variable to the point of being entirely absent in some mothers. It is clear that in order for a mother to reinforce, she must be both near and attentive, but she need not be affectionate. Some mothers are not characteristically affectionate, and their children should be quite unresponsive to affection. However, they may be well reinforced by both the proximity and attention of adults. The literature of clinical child psychology is rich in descriptions of children who are "social," in that they are extremely sensitive to having an audience, but "psychopathic," in that the respect or affection of that audience is entirely without value to them. Such a child might well have a history in which displays of affection were never discriminative for other reinforcers.

For children with mothers who have made their affection discriminative to the baby for the other reinforcers in caretaking activities, affection operates as a positive reinforcer. It serves as an important stimulus in the developing behavior of these children because it is not ordinarily used to strengthen bad behavior (as attention and proximity often are). The mother may not be able to avoid attending to the baby's undesirable behavior, bringing herself in close proximity to him, but she is unlikely to meet it with affection. In fact, she is much more likely to cease all displays of affection on occasions that displease her. Because the withdrawal or loss of a positive reinforcer acts to weaken any preceding operant behavior, bad behaviors may be weakened more by the mother's withdrawal of affection than they are strengthened through her attention.

The ease of giving affection for good behavior, and the natural tendency not to present it and to withdraw it when confronted with bad behavior, set up situations which strengthen selectively those behaviors which please the mother, rather than those which displease her. This line of reasoning suggests that children who are maximally responsive to affection as a positive reinforcer are more readily influenced by the mother's goals for them than are children more responsive to her attention than to her affection.

REFERENCES

Brackbill, Yvonne. Extinction of the smiling response in infants as a function of reinforcement schedule. *Child Develpm.*, 1958, *29*, 115–124.

Gewirtz, J. L. Three determinants of attention-seeking in young children. *Monog. Soc. Res. Child Developm.*, 1954, *19*, no. 2.

Gewirtz, J. L. A learning analysis of the effects of normal stimulation, privation and deprivation on the acquisition of social motivation and attachment. In B. M. Moss (Ed.) *Determinants of infant behavior.* New York: Wiley, 1961.

Gibson, J. M. *The perception of the visual world.* Boston: Houghton Mifflin, 1950.

9

The Development of Perceiving Behavior to Physical Stimuli

INTRODUCTION

By the end of the Universal stage, the baby's behavior has become extensively developed and elaborated. Many forms of behavior now characterize an organism originally describable by a rather modest list (cf. Chapter 3). Similarly, the stimuli controlling these expanded repertories are correspondingly numerous. Thus, by the end of the Universal stage it is practically impossible to find in the baby's repertory an *un*differentiated, *un*discriminated operant.

In this chapter, a further application of the principles of differentiation, discrimination, and chaining will be made, one which suggests further elaboration of behavior to physical stimuli commonly called "perceptual." The conversion of the amorphous, unshaped operant behavior of an infant into a large set of differentiated, discriminated operants sets the stage for the development of still further differentiation of new operant behavior, which in turn will come under the control of new discriminative stimuli.

This line of development follows from the principles of differentiation, discrimination, and, especially, acquired reinforcement. To form a discriminative operant is to give some stimulus control over the response. That is, the response has a different strength in the presence of one discriminative stimulus than it has in the presence of all others. This characteristic of an operant response is possible only if the stimuli involved serve as cues for certain reinforcement, punishment, or extinction contingencies in which the response is involved. For example, a baby may fuss a good deal of the time in the presence of his father because his father frequently responds with attention, cuddling, or other demonstrations of concern. The baby's fussing may occur only at low, operant level in the presence of his mother if she consistently pays no attention to it (unless it is a genuine cry of pain, hunger, cold, etc., which she discriminates from operant fussing). With his dog, the baby may not fuss at all, because the dog always responds to fussing with extensive licking of the baby's face (a negative reinforcer for many children). So it can be seen that there are at least three stimuli with discriminative functions for fussing in this baby's life: the presence of the father produces it with high frequency; the presence of the mother reduces it to its operant level; the presence of the dog eliminates or actively suppresses it. Each stimulus has a strength-changing function because each is discriminative for a difference consequence of the response: positive reinforcers, neutral stimuli, and negative reinforcers, respectively.

As noted previously, a stimulus with a discriminative function is also a stimulus with a reinforcing function. Its reinforcing function may be positive or negative, depending on the kind of contingency with which the stimulus has been associated. Discriminative stimuli associated with the presentation of positive reinforcers or the removal of negative reinforcers take on a positive reinforcing function; discriminative stimuli associated with the addition of negative reinforcers or the removal of positive reinforcers take on a negative reinforcing function.

If these stimuli acquire new reinforcing properties, they function to differentiate new operant behaviors in the baby. Positive reinforcers strengthen responses that produce them and weaken responses that lose them. Negative reinforcers weaken responses that produce them and strengthen responses that avoid them.

What are these newly differentiated responses likely to be? In principle, they can be any operant behaviors which circumstances allow to fall into regular or at least occasional contingency with these new reinforcers. However, a certain class of new behaviors are highly probable. These are responses which orient the receptors toward stimuli; they would be "discriminative stimulus-seeking" behaviors, or "discriminative stimulus-avoiding" behaviors. Among the effective ways of "seeking" discriminative stimuli are looking, listening, and feeling responses; among those to "avoid" discriminative stimuli are looking elsewhere, "not attending," and "minding your own business" behaviors.

These may be called "attending behaviors" and may be analyzed as operant responses whose only function is to either maximize or minimize stimulus input (especially, discriminative stimulus input) to the child. These responses are typically simple motor behaviors: coordinated motions of the eyes in scanning the environment or in fixing on an object, cocking the head to turn the ears toward sources of sounds, reaching out to touch surfaces with fingers or palms, etc. Sometimes such behaviors involve more complex chains, such as shielding the eyes from interfering bright lights to see more clearly, or asking others to be quiet so that one can hear better. In other words, there is a turning away from distracting sources of stimulation of any kind. Some forms of this behavior may be even more complex, such as when a baby places his toys in appropriate containers to be able to find certain ones more easily at a later time. (Libraries do much the same with card files.)

There is more. We present the further elaboration in the form of a concrete example around which our discussion will be organized:

A two-year-old is playing with his mother in the front yard of their home. A car horn sounds on the child's left. He turns his head toward the left, his eyes moving in that direction until he sees the car. As the car drives by him, passing from left to right, the child's head also turns from left to right. Then he says, "Look, it's a car!" to which his mother replies, "Yes, a car."

The above represents the organization of behavior into a *chain*. The chain is composed of stimuli and responses, in which each stimulus sets the occasion for the following response, and each response produces a new stimulus which in turn sets the occasion for the next response. In our example, the chain begins with the sound of the car's horn. The sound has the discriminative function for a sweeping response of the eyes toward the left to where the car horn is. The youngster's past history of reinforcement has been such that when sounds strike his ears with the phase and intensity difference just experienced, a left sweep of the eyes is more likely to produce a discriminative stimulus than a right sweep. (Had the phasing of the sound to the ears been opposite, the child would have looked to the right.) In other words, the child has already experienced a great deal of relevant discrimination and differentiation training. Responses in one direction have been differentially strengthened under certain arrangements of sounds; responses in the other direction have been strengthened under other arrangements of the sounds. These responses might be termed "locating" or "looking-for" behavior. Their only distinctive characteristic is that they are responses yielding a discriminative stimulus for the next response in the chain. This stimulus is the sight of the car which adds a visual component to the child's stimulus input, in addition to the auditory stimulus to which he is already responding.

For a two-year-old, the sound of a car horn may not be sufficient to produce the discriminated verbal operant, "Look, it's a car!" Actually seeing the car is undoubtedly sufficient. For a two-year-old, it may well be that a mere glimpse is not enough to discriminate the car from other objects; several seconds of inspection may be necessary. The head and eyes may continue sweeping left and right while the car moves across the child's field of vision. The car's movement is a discriminative stimulus to the child for a corresponding movement with eyes and head to keep the car fixed in his vision. Such visual tracking is a pattern of interaction which the child has been practicing since the first few days after birth; by now it is a well-discriminated and differentiated skill. As the child continues to look at the car, additional looking may produce a variety of detailed stimuli: general shape and size, wheels, windows, person inside—enough stimuli, finally, to produce the verbal response "car." Having his mother present (another discriminative stimulus), he makes an audible verbal response, prefaced by "Look, it's a . . ." "Look, it's a car!" is a verbal response more appropriate in the presence of mother, because she may give a verbal (social) reinforcer in turn, if she is properly addressed, for example, with "Look." In this child's history, it is probable that "Look, it's a . . ." has more often commanded an adult's response than simply naming the sighted object.

In the above example, it might seem that the child attended to the car simply to name it for his doting mother and thus receive a social reinforcer, since the chain ended with a social reinforcer. The possibility is not unrealistic. A child may attend to an event merely to label it for an appreciative audience. The ability to talk is one of the most exciting developments that children show, and most adult audiences reinforce it to a high degree. However, even if his mother had not been present, the child might have turned his head to pinpoint the sound and might have continued to view the car, even though the chain could not have terminated in a social reinforcer; a car is a discriminative stimulus, so seeing it reinforces looking behavior.

Why does the child bother to attend, locate and identify an object, without any promise of extrinsic reinforcement? The example shows a fundamental characteristic of such behavior: *sometimes* it contributes to chains that terminate in reinforcement. The typical inconsistencies of the environment suggest that such reinforcement will be intermittent. In everyday life, the schedule must be rich enough to both shape and maintain the behavior of attending to discriminative stimuli. Indeed, an intermittent schedule will make these behaviors durable and widely generalized. The child may well continue to attend to, locate, examine, or notice events in the environment simply because to do so often creates a chain ending in reinforcement. In terms of economics, it pays to keep your eyes open. In technical terms, a child's world abounds with positive reinforcers which can be had readily if only they are noticed, and with negative reinforcers which can be avoided easily if only they are noticed in time. Either kind of contingency can be sufficient to set up a high rate of attending to the details of the environment.

It is often claimed that a formulation in terms of operant chains is adequate for an analysis of simple learning, discrimination, and even concept formation, but not for perceptual behavior. For this reason, it will be relevant to present a brief account of the older approaches to these phenomena before elaborating further on the analysis advanced here.

THE CONCEPT OF SENSATION AND PERCEPTION

To say that our analysis of the development of behavior to physical stimuli includes perceiving behavior is to encompass a tremendous expanse of psychological territory, for it is in this region that such questions as these are typically posed: How does the infant come to know, be aware of, and understand the way the physical world is organized? How does he come to make meaningful "wholes" out of a welter of haphazard physical stimuli? How does the infant's mental structure (which is obviously internal) come to know the nature of the physical world (which is obviously external)?

These questions are difficult not only because of the complex nature of the inter-relationships involved but also because of the inclusion of assumptions incompatible with a natural science study of behavior. The point relative to complexity is apparent; the one relative to incompatibility with a natural science approach may not be. Let us therefore begin an elaboration of the incompatibility aspect by pointing out that questions of this sort assume a relationship between the individual and the physical world which consists of three interconnected phases: (1) reception of stimulation from the physical environment and its movement to some central point or process, (2) integration and interpretation of stimulus input with other stimulus variables derived from the history of the person and the current situation, and (3) transformation of the interpreted stimulus into action on the physical environment. Each phase will be considered in turn.

An analysis of the reception of stimulus input might explore the relationships between stimulus properties and the indications of qualitative and quantitative changes in "sensations." In such a treatment sensations might be defined as "primitive activities resulting from contacts with physical stimuli and mediated by the sense organ with little if any interpretation by the central nervous system" (Thompson, p. 317–318) or as "simple elements which go to make up wholes that we call objects" (Woodworth and Schlosberg, 1954, p. 293).

It should be apparent that information about the "sensation" is derived from a psychological response (response of the total organism), usually in a verbal form. The assumption that sensations are simple sensory reactions is difficult to integrate with a natural science point of view. What is referred to as "an act of receiving sensations" is operant behavior. As operant behavior its occurrence or non-occurrence or its strength at any time is a function of reinforcement history, motivational operations, emotional conditions, instructions, and other setting events. Reactions to physical events can be analyzed like other operant behavior and require no unique principles. This point will be discussed further in the next section dealing with stimulus-response interaction chains.

In passing it should be pointed out that an analysis of the reception of stimulation from the physical environment need not be concerned with the nature of the sensations produced but rather with the changes that take place in the sense organs. Sense organ structure and functioning with respect to variations in stimulation delineates the field of sensory physiology, or a part of the field of physiological psychology or psychophysiology. Investigations in this area may be concerned with the way the pupil of the eye contracts with increases in illumination, or the way the rod and cone cells of the retina function with changes of visual stimuli from non-chroma to chroma, or the way the membranes in the cochlea vary with sound frequency at a given decibel level of intensity. Although such studies have as their goal the exploration of relationships between stimulus dimensions and sense organ characteristics, this branch of research is often referred to as the "biology of attending."

The second phase of the perceptual process—the process by which sensations are integrated with other variables and emerge in meaningful form—is often viewed as: (1) brain and central nervous system activity, (2) a network of purely hypothetical variables, or (3) a combination of both. For example, Thompson (1962) says: ". . . perceptions are the results of interactions between sensory and central nervous system processes, sensory data 'interpreted' within the matrix of present neurological processes, current motivating conditions, and a variety of other psychological variables" (p. 318).

In light of our knowledge of neurology, attributing the integrative or interpretive aspect of the perceptual process to the brain and central nervous system is a highly dubious practice. It is clear that the brain and central nervous system serve to coordinate neurological impulses. The possibility that they also serve to transform sensations of elementary sensory experiences into something meaningful, or indeed into "meaning" itself, seems exceedingly remote: the equation of "meaning" into neural terms is at best an arbitrary process of definition, rather than of analysis.

Another approach to the study of the integrative or interpretive process replaces central nervous system activity with hypothetical terms, a solution which presents another difficulty. How, for example, can the investigator know the nature of these hypothetical variables and the way they interact with each other? One answer is: by the use of inference based on what the child does and says, especially in response to relevant questions. By this procedure the investigator can determine what the physical world means to the child; he can "see" the child's physical world "through the child's eyes."

Obviously, the potentiality of this point of view, known as the phenomenological approach, rests on the validity of the inferential procedure involved. On this score, the procedure is less than sound for it merely assigns another name to the behavior observed, and the name assigned is said to be a causal variable. For example, asking a four-year-old why he persists in pulling the cat's tail might produce the answer: "Because I want to see how loud he can holler."

Phenomenologically, this response might be taken to mean that the child *perceived* the cat as an object for satisfying his curiosity or his exploratory needs. Obviously, this "explanation" provides no new information about the independent variables that might be involved in producing and maintaining tail-pulling behavior in the youngster. On the other hand, an objective and experimental analysis might show that, in this particular case, if we instruct the child's audience to pay no attention to his mauling the cat, then the behavior will extinguish in short order. In other words, observation indicates that the behavior is reinforced by attention. Further manipulation of the child's environmental variables might show that often the attention secured by this response turns into disapproval, but that a disapproving adult can be disarmed by the verbal operant, "To see how loud he can holler," which removes disapproval and produces laughter in the attending adult. In another case, we might find that the responses of adults to the same behavior are unimportant, but that if the cat is anesthetized and so becomes completely unresponsive, then the child's behavior extinguishes, no matter what adult responses to the behavior might be. In this case, it is indeed the cat's response which is maintaining the child's behavior. We might then selectively change the cat (make him responsive but mute, or make him vocal but immobile) to analyze more specifically just what part of the cat's response to the child is the functional stimulus. But in any case, it should be apparent that *actual* analysis of the relevant stimulus functions is more informative, and more likely accurate, than *inferential* analysis. And it should also be apparent that actual analysis, with observable stimulus and response events, is possible—there is no necessity to infer.

The third phase of the perceptual process is that concerned with how the product of the interpretive process is transformed into action. This action may range widely, from a simple response to a complex sequence involving social, emotional, and intellectual interactions. Analyses are made in terms of either hypothetical neurological processes or of hypothetical unspecified variables, similar to the treatment of the first two phases of the assumed perceptual processes. Thus, counter-argument and query would again be similar.

STIMULUS-RESPONSE INTERACTIONAL CHAINS

An alternate view of perceiving behavior is one which conceives of the perceptual process as a somewhat specialized series of stimulus-response interactions between a total functioning biological organism and physical events (Goldiamond, 1962; Schoenfeld and Cummings, 1963; Skinner, 1953 and 1963). The specialized series of interactions is typically an operant chain. Operant chains, it will be recalled, are sequences in which a discriminative stimulus is followed by a differentiated response producing a discriminative stimulus for another differentiated response leading in turn to a reinforcement.

We can, for the sake of convenience, describe the first part of such a chain as *coming into contact with a discriminative stimulus,* or as attending behavior. In many instances, behavior which maintains contact, once established, is also part of the attending act. Other terms such as sensing, detecting, locating, stimulus-actualizing, and receptor-orienting behavior have been used. The second part of the sequence may be analyzed as *discriminative behavior to the stimuli controlling the behavior of the individual* and might be called the perceiving behavior. "Seeing" and "knowing" are also frequently used terms. The third segment of the chain may also be described as discriminative behavior, but in this link it is *discriminative behavior in relation to stimuli from the previous discriminative act,* or reporting behavior.

Let us return to the example of the two-year-old playing with his mother in the front yard of their home when a car approaches and the horn is sounded. The sound of the horn is the "new" stimulus. The child turns his head, eyes, and body and sees the object making the sound. This is the attending or orienting act. The stimulus-complex, the car, reinforces the orienting behavior in relation to sounds of this sort, and also sets the occasion for discriminating them in some detail.

It cannot be assumed that because a child is oriented to an identifiable source of stimulation he is actually engaging in attending behavior with respect to that stimulus (any more than a student's moving his eyes along a line of print guarantees that he is "reading"); or that when a child who is apparently not oriented toward a discernible stimulus is not participating in attending behavior relative to it. The only way to tell whether he is actualizing a stimulus is to demonstrate that his behavior is in fact controlled by the stimulus, that is, variations in the behavior are functionally related to variations in the stimulus event. This criterion is the same as for any functional relationship. For example, it may be recalled that the criterion for a reinforcing stimulus is a demonstration that, on subsequent occasions, a response in the response class which preceded it is strengthened.

Attending behavior consists not of stimulus inputs but of specific muscle functions. Like other discriminative operants, their exact form and strength depend upon the reinforcement history in similar circumstances, the characteristics of the stimulus occasion, current motivational and emotional conditions, and other setting events.

The second part of the chain, the perceiving part, is a three-term contingency involving first an actualized stimulus functioning as the discriminative stimulus, second a differentiated behavior consisting of subtle components such as surveying, comparing, and contrasting, and third, an acquired reinforcing stimulus.

In the example, the perceiving behavior consists of the child's surveying the size, color, shape, composition, and other details of the car, the activities of the driver, etc., and of his making some sort of a final response that may or may not be directly observable. To *know what this stimulus-complex "means" to the child is to observe what he says or what he does with respect to it.* These actions constitute the next link.

Part three of the chain refers to "reporting behavior" and consists of differentiated behavior with respect to stimuli generated by the final act of the second link. Depending on circumstances, the individual may respond to his own behavior with verbal behaviors that name, describe, classify, conceptualize, and so on (called "tacting" behavior in chapter 10); or may engage in nonverbal behavior relative to other stimulus events. The latter might range from making previously learned responses, to solving new problems.

In the example, the child reacts to visual stimuli generated by the final behavior of the "perceiving" link with a statement categorizing the object, "Look, it's a car." Such a statement would be taken to mean that for him it is an object similar to others, that vary in stimulus properties over a wide range from trailer-trucks to sassy sports cars, but different from others that move about such as airplanes and trains. The mother's "Yes" probably helps him to categorize future stimuli along these dimensions.

As is true of responses in the first and second links, what the child says or does in this phase is a function of the reinforcement and discriminative stimulus histories and the relevant variables in the current situation, including motivational, emotional conditions, and other setting events. Obviously if the child had a history completely devoid of experiences with cars or even pictures of them, then he could hardly be expected to say, "Look, it's a car." On the other hand, if he were in a different situation, say alone (rather than with his mother), then he would not be likely to report the object—at least not aloud. He might instead run to the car, if it stops, and examine it or respond to the driver.

ANTECEDENT AND INITIAL PHASES OF PERCEIVING BEHAVIOR

Let us now turn to a consideration of the evolution of perceiving behavior, of how these special chains become established. The antecedent and initial phases of perceiving behavior generate from progressive changes in interactions between the organism and the environment, in this case the physical environment. Such transformations probably start as unconditioned and nondiscriminated reactions to restricted ranges of physical stimuli. Through selective reinforcement differentiated reactions develop to extended ranges and to detailed aspects of physical stimuli. Next come differentiated reactions to stimuli generated by discriminative reactions to physical stimuli.

Unconditioned and Nondiscriminated Reactions to Restricted Ranges of Physical Stimuli

The infant's initial contacts with the physical environment are undoubtedly his unconditioned and nondiscriminated reactions to stimuli, mostly at the stronger intensity ranges. In chapter 3 it was pointed out that knowledge about the sensitivities of the newborn rests upon demonstrable correlations between stimuli and dependable response measures. Research findings suggest that during the first post-natal month the infant responds to the stronger intensities of lights, sounds, odors, pressures, electric stimulation, body movements, and chemical substances on the tongue and other surfaces of the body. He also responds to variations in the upper and lower temperature ranges (Jensen, 1932).

Reactions to such stimuli are several. First, there are changes in undifferentiated bodily activities and accompanying changes in physiological functioning, particularly in the respiratory and cardiac systems. The magnitude of such behavior changes is roughly related to the intensity in one or more of the stimulus dimensions noted, at least up to the onset of full-blown crying behavior. Second, there appear to be fairly precise unconditioned responses to specific stimuli. For example, movements of an attractive object across the visual field produce eye-tracking and correlated head-turning behaviors; three-dimensional objects and patterned designs produce longer visual fixations than do two-dimensional drawings and less patterned designs (Fantz, 1958 and 1961). There is a third class of responses: the specific behaviors to specific stimulation, mostly on the surface of the body, for example. Since these responses are not modifiable by conditioning procedures, they are classified as biological rather than psychological, and are not included in this summary.

It was noted earlier that repeated presentations of a stimulus to a newborn tend to reduce the power of that stimulus; that is to say, response strength decreases as stimulations follow one another in rapid succession. Under these circumstances, adaptation is said to have occurred. The variables in adaptation have not as yet been fully analyzed (Lipsitt, 1963) mainly because this phenomenon has been looked upon as merely an obstruction to investigating respondent conditioning in the neonate. Perhaps adaptation takes place during this period not only because of the immaturity of the biological structure and functioning of the infant but also because of (1) the absence of essential consequent stimuli to maintaining behavior, and (2) the presence of strong and persistent competition from biological processes, e.g., digestion, sleep, and fatigue cycles.

Differentiated Reactions to Extended Ranges and to Detailed Aspects of Physical Stimuli

Through selective reinforcement, differentiated and discriminated reactions develop to stimuli over wider ranges made possible by increased biological maturation. Objects differing in form (Ling, 1941), color (Staples, 1932; Simons and Lipsitt, 1961), and localization (Munn, 1965) become discriminative stimuli for responses followed by the presentation and withdrawal of positive and negative reinforcers.

Through the same process, reactions come under the control of one or a combination of several dimensions or components of a complex stimulus. For this kind of discriminative behavior which is often called abstracting behavior to come into existence, it is necessary that the mother, father, and other members of the family arrange antecedent and consequent stimuli so that responses to the critical dimension of a stimulus (e.g., its triangularity feature) are systematically reinforced and responses to all the other dimensions (e.g., its size, color, location, and spatial orientation) are regularly followed by neutral or aversive consequences. Effective training of this sort (learning to abstract) enables the child to make common verbal (e.g., naming "triangle") and nonverbal responses (e.g., approaching in a similar manner) to stimuli that are grossly dissimilar, that is, to engage in conceptualizing behavior. Although some forms of conceptualizing behavior are established near the end of the Universal stage, most of them begin to develop in the Basic stage and thereafter increase in large increments. The onset and exercise of verbal facility ordinarily acquired after the Universal stage play a substantial role in building serviceable conceptualizing repertories.

Much of the experimental work on the beginnings of such discriminative behavior (e.g., reactions to stimulus objects at a distance, or "depth perception") has been concerned with whether it is initially a learned or an unlearned act. More recently, however, there has been less concern over the heredity-versus-environment issue and more interest in describing the exact responses involved and in examining almost microscopically the historical and current conditions influencing behavioral changes and the rate and order of their progression.

Another substantial segment of research in discriminative behavior to physical stimuli is normative in nature. Normative research, it will be recalled, aims to establish the average age at which certain classes of behavior appear. For example, norms may be established to show the average age at which an infant discriminates a circular object from a retangular block, or a red from a green patch of paper, or when he can orient his head and eyes with fair accuracy to a sound source.

Although the research in the development of discriminative repertories has been divided into experimental and normative studies, the two types of investigations are not necessarily unrelated. In fact, normative studies may pave the way for functional studies. A good example is the research of Gibson and her coworkers on the development of differential behavior to a "visual cliff" (1963). Normative research was conducted to determine at what ages human and infrahuman subjects, when placed on a center platform between a shallow drop-off and a deep drop-off (covered with glass), would cross over the "deep" side. Subsequently, experimental studies were conducted to determine the role of differences in surfaces and textures of the floor of the deep side of the "visual cliff."

Differentiated Reactions to Stimuli Generated by Discriminative Reactions to Physical Stimuli

The development of differentiated reactions to stimuli from discriminative reactions to physical stimuli is probably only minimally established during the Universal stage. The language facility developed and maintained after the Universal period plays an essential function. Hence, analysis of the development of further differentiated reactions to the stimuli generated by perceiving behavior to physical stimuli will be more appropriately presented in Volume 3. It need only be pointed out here that such an analysis is critical to a consideration of complex behavioral processes (such as reasoning, problem-solving, and thinking) that are so much in evidence during later development.

REFERENCES

Fantz, R. L. Visual discrimination in young infants. *Psychol. Rec.*, 1958, *8*, 43–47.

Fantz, R. L. The origin of form perception. *Scient. Amer.*, 1961, 204, No. 5, 66–72.

Gibson, Eleanor J. Perceptual development. In H. W. Stevenson (Ed.), *Child Psychology.* The sixty-second Yearbook of the National Society for the Study of Education, Part I. Chicago: Univ. of Chicago Press, 1963.

Goldiamond, I. Perception. In A. Bachrach (Ed.), *Experimental foundations of clinical psychology.* New York: Basic Books, 1962.

Jensen, K. Differential reactions to taste and temperature stimuli in newborn infants. *Genet. Psychol. Monogr.*, 1932, *12*, 361–479.

Ling, B-C. Form discrimination as a learning cue in infants. *Comp. Psychol. Monogr.*, 1941, *17*, No. 2.

Lipsitt, L. P. Learning in the first year of life. In L. P. Lipsitt and C. C. Spike (Eds.), *Advances in child development and behavior.* Vol. I, New York: Academic Press, 1963.

Munn, N. L. *The evolution and growth of human behavior.* (2nd ed.) New York: Houghton Mifflin, 1965.

Schoenfeld, W. N., and Cumming, W. W. Behavior and perception. In S. Koch (Ed.), *Psychology: A study of a science.* Vol. 5. New York: McGraw-Hill, 1963.

Simmons, Mae W., and Lipsitt, L. P. An operant discrimination apparatus for infants. *J. exp. anal. Behav.*, 1961, *4*, 233–235.

Skinner, B. F. *Science and human behavior.* New York: Macmillan, 1953.

Skinner, B. F. *Behaviorism at fifty.* Science, 1963, *140*, 951–958.

Staples, R. The responses of infants to color. *J. exp. Psychol.*, 1932, *15*, 119–141.

Thompson, G. *Child Psychology: Growth trends in psychological adjustment.* (2nd Ed.) Boston: Houghton Mifflin, 1962.

Woodworth, R. S., and Schlosberg, H. *Experimental psychology.* (Rev. ed.) New York: Holt, 1954.

10

The Onset and Beginnings of Verbal Behavior

This chapter is a continuation of the theme begun in Chapter 5: immediately after birth the baby acts on his environment and changes it, and in so doing his own behavior is changed. As in Chapter 7, the emphasis here is on how the form of behavior is modified. This time, however, the behavior under scrutiny is verbal in nature.

Philosophers and scientists have said many things about the significance of language in the evolution and current status of man. Little more need be added. However, the role of language in man's conception of man might be emphasized by a hypothetical situation. Suppose you were suddenly confronted with an ape who was perfectly capable of telling you, in good English, his past history, his future plans, and what he claimed were his innermost thoughts and feelings. Suppose further that he were thoroughly competent in carrying on a give-and-take conversation in practically any subject you chose to discuss. Would you, after such an encounter, treat him as a human being or as an ape? Would you, for example, help him find a comfortable place to live, one in which he might carry on an independent existence, or would you pack him off to the zoo? It would be difficult to decide. Language does, indeed, give man one of his most distinctive characteristics. (Perhaps the fact that man is a culture-building animal gives him his second most distinctive characteristic. The two are not unrelated.)

Let us clarify the meaning of two terms which will be central in our discussion:

1. *Vocal behavior.* This term refers to the behavior involved in producing sounds with the vocal apparatus. The sound-making mechanism includes the diaphragm, the vocal cords, the false vocal cords, the epiglottis, the soft palate, the tongue, the cheek, the lips, and the jaw. The acoustical products generated may be studied in three interrelated ways: (1) in terms of relationships between sounds produced and activities in the anatomy and physiology of the vocal apparatus; (2) in terms of changes in the physical and social environments; and (3) in terms of normative patterns of change in sounds produced and expansion over time as the infant ages. The first area is usually referred to as developmental phonetics and is exemplified in the literature of child development by the work of Irwin (1941). The second is usually designated as functional analysis; it is exemplified by the analyses of Skinner (1957) and Osgood (1953). The third is generally categorized as normative or longitudinal analysis. McCarthy offers a thorough review of the techniques used and their results (1954). Our concern here is primarily with a functional analysis of vocal productions, or how vocalizations acquire their response functions.

2. *Verbal behavior.* This concept refers to vocal behavior reinforced through the mediation of another person. It follows from this definition that verbal behavior is one class of social behavior, but social behavior is not restricted to verbal behavior. Included in social behavior are gestures, facial expressions, body postures, sign language, written materials, signals, and the like. In fact, any action on the part of one individual which can be shown to affect the action of another individual would be included.

Our definition also excludes as verbal behavior all noises by the individual which do not involve his vocal apparatus and all sounds generated through the vocal apparatus that are functionally related to antecedent stimulation (respondent vocalization), such as coughing because of a throat irritation.

Verbal behavior, then, designates that class of vocal behavior that is reinforced through the action of another person, whether the other person's behavior is itself the reinforcing contingency (such as paying attention) or the person's behavior results in producing some other contingency (such as an ice cream cone).

DEVELOPMENT OF INITIAL VERBAL BEHAVIOR

The mother's vocal behavior is usually mixed with her proximity, attention, and affection. The interweaving of these stimuli comes about in at least three ways. First, she does not usually speak to the baby unless she is sufficiently near to be heard. Second, she is accustomed to speaking to others (her husband, older children, relatives, and friends) while attending to their needs and so it is likely that she will talk to the baby while attending to his needs. (Under these circumstances the mother is reacting to discriminative stimuli which have gained power through generalization since the baby will never have reinforced her for talking to him.) Third, many mothers use pet names and endearing phrases in displaying affection. So it follows that as the proximity, attention, and affection of the mother are discriminative stimuli for the reinforcement procedures inherent in caretaking and child-rearing, so is the auditory stimulation she provides.

A baby can produce such auditory stimulation in two ways: (1) he can provoke others into speaking to him, or (2) he can make these sounds himself, with his own vocal apparatus. The first way includes behaviors by the baby like smiling, waving ("bye-bye"), hand-clapping ("pattycake"), toddling toward the mother, and vocalizing in the presence of people. The second way is vocalization by the baby. The normal baby hears his own vocalization, of course. Such sounds are mildly reinforcing in that they function like other ecological reinforcers. They gain additional reinforcing effectiveness, however, if they are similar to the mother's vocalizations (generalization). Hence one might say that the sound of the baby's vocalizations "automatically" strengthens the vocalizations themselves. As a result, the infant's vocal responses become both stronger and differentiated into those which more and more closely produce sounds like the mother's speech, since vocal responses which resemble the mother's will be strengthened more than vocal responses which do not.

This process has been described in detail by many psychologists. Osgood (1953), for example, has not only brought much of this data together but also has presented a set of labels for describing stages in this line of development. His characterization of the vocal sounds produced during the first few months of life emphasizes their *random nature,* noting that the vocal apparatus "is a muscular system, and activity here partakes of the gross, mass activity of the total organism. Just as arms and legs are randomly moved about, so the jaws, lips, tongue, and vocal cords are randomly exercised, and when air happens to be pushed through the oral cavity, varying patterns of sound are produced" (p. 684). Following through on this type of analysis, the initial vocal behavior of the infant may be viewed in terms of operant interactions.

Osgood notes that random vocal responding is composed of a great variety of sounds:

> . . . Within the data for the first two months of life may be found all of the speech sounds that the human vocal system can produce, including French vowel and trills, German umlaut and guttural sounds, and many that are only describable in phonetic symbols. This is in flat contradiction to the notion that the infant gradually "becomes capable" of making various sounds (p. 684).

The view that the infant makes more and more new sounds as he matures had been the accepted way of thinking about the development of speech sound units or *phonemes*. As Osgood points out, the discrepancy in points of view is probably due to the inadequate methods of speech recording previously used. Modern tape recordings which allow detailed and repeated study of the infant's speech sounds are said to bear out Osgood's claim.

> A more accurate statement would be that the comparative *frequencies* of various speech sounds change as development proceeds; owing to a number of anatomical factors, there is variation in the *probability* of given combinations of jaw, lip, and tongue positions being assumed (and hence the probability of various sounds being produced) (*op. cit.*, pp. 684–685).

Coupled with this extensive output of operant verbal behavior are respondent vocalizations, such as crying under conditions of distress involving negative reinforcement and loss of positive reinforcement, and uttering soft, open vowel sounds when positive reinforcers are presented. Both classes of behavior undergo considerable modification with increasing development, but the most marked changes occur in operant vocalization. Respondent vocalizations elicited by reinforcement operations characterize the adult as well as the infant, but in the adult they are not as readily evoked or as intense in expression.

The operant component of speech sounds becomes shaped into the language of the culture. The initial step is accomplished by the differential strengthening of these vocalizations which produce reinforcers. One class of reinforcers, as we have seen, is the sounds of the baby's vocalizations which resemble the sounds made by the mother. Other reinforcers usually include the mother's delighted and affectionate attention, attracted by speechlike utterances of the baby which are sometimes referred to as *morphemes,* the combination of sounds with "meaning." In either contingency, an increasingly speech-like quality is differentially strengthened. The result is a gradual transition from random sounds to syllabic arrangements of the sounds characteristic of the mother's vocal behavior.

This course of development continues steadily, increasing in both the range and the rate of syllabic utterances, suggesting the term *syllabic babbling* as a description of the behavior. One description of the sounds produced by babbling includes such phrases as "uggle-uggle," "a-bah-bah," "bup-bup-bup," "aduh-ajuh," and "lul-lul-lah" (Shirley, 1933). Clearly, these sounds resemble adult speech more than the isolated, shorter sounds of earlier months.

Since the process for producing and maintaining syllabic babbling is largely the action of self-reinforcement supported by the mother's speech, babbling behaviors increase in strength, variety, and chained sequences. As these interactions proceed, the baby becomes more accurate in mimicry skills, and more likely to mimic the sounds just heard. To babble is to make responses which produce reinforcing sounds. These sounds not only reinforce the vocal apparatus responses which produced them, but they also become discriminative for continuation and for receiving further reinforcement. Consequently, babbling takes on a chained aspect, the same and different sounds being linked in longer and longer sequences. Mothers often encourage such chaining by mimicking their baby's babbling, prompting the baby to repeat it. In this way, a sound made by the mother sets the occasion for the emission of sound by her baby, and the more similar the baby's sound is to the mother's, the more self-reinforcing it is for the baby. Thus, this interaction between the mother and the baby develops in the baby a vocal repertory which contains more and more accurate copies of adult speech sounds, each more and more discriminated to occasions when others make the same sounds. In short, the baby's babbling has become largely *imitation* of speech sounds (Osgood, 1953) or *echoic* (Skinner, 1957).

The development of imitative babbling thus lays the groundwork for *labeling*. One method of accomplishing labeling is to show the baby the object to be labeled—for example, a cat—and at the same time say its name repeatedly—"Kitty, kitty, kitty." Responding at first to the sounds of these words, the child imitates, perhaps with "Kid-dee, kid-dee, kid-dee." Usually the mother reinforces this response differentially with attention; approval, such as "Good," "Fine," and "That's right"; and other reinforcers (depending, of course, upon her current enthusiasm for this kind of development in her child). Thus "kid-dee" would become discriminated, if these contingencies are repeated often enough, not only to the sound "kitty" which initially prompts the response, but to the presence of the cat as well. In the presence of the cat (the discriminative stimulus) the young child comes to respond verbally with "kid-dee" (the discriminated operant) and be reinforced. It is less likely that the young child would be reinforced if he made the same response in the absence of the cat.

The reinforcers in the example above will most frequently be social (signs of approval, etc.), in which case the operant qualifies as an example of a *tact* (Skinner, 1957). "A tact may be defined as a verbal operant in which a response of a given form is evoked (or at least strengthened) by a particular object or event or property of an object or event. W account for the strength by showing that in the presence of the object or event a response of that form is characteristically reinforced in a given verbal community" (Skinner, 1957, pp. 81–82). The contingency usually involves generalized reinforcers such as "Good," "Fine," or "That's right," mentioned above.

By contrast, some verbalizations of the baby are uttered because they are characteristically brought about by the listener. For example, the baby may have learned to say "doo-dee" in relation to cookies, not so much because of the social reinforcers previously received for correct labeling but primarily for the cookie he acquires when he so utters these sounds. In this case the verbalization is called a *mand* (Skinner, 1957). Mands, which make up a class of verbal response functions, are usually uttered in the relevant deprivation state (such as lack of food) or aversive stimulation rather than in the presence of the object itself, and are reinforced by an appropriate event or object (the cookie) more than by consequent generalized social reinforcement.

As the infant increases his skills in labeling things he increases the degree of control over that part of his world which his mother provides for him. Some of that world is the social reinforcement she makes available to him; some is the physical reinforcement which she arranges. In either event, a social contingency is implicit in the development. Thus verbal development is both a product of social interactions and a producer of equipment which enables the baby to engage in more social behavior.

STUDIES OF THE FUNCTIONAL ASPECTS OF THE VERBAL BEHAVIOR OF INFANTS

Because of the difficulties involved, there are only a few studies illustrating the role of social reinforcers in the verbal behavior of infants. Despite the limitations imposed on conducting such research, however, it is not impossible, and because of the importance of such information it seems likely that much more research of this type will be conducted in the near future, even with very young babies.

Among the youngest babies whose verbal behavior has been studied are the three-month-olds of Rheingold, Gewirtz, and Ross (1959). The experimental question was: Do vocalizations of young infants have operant properties? Because of their belief that vocalization provided an index of the socialization process, they used social reinforcement which "an attentive adult might naturally make when a child vocalizes" (p. 68). Clearly, the response had to be judged as such by the investigator doing the reinforcing. On those occasions when the response was ambiguous or otherwise difficult to judge, reinforcement was probably delayed and sometimes incorrectly administered. This disadvantage is probably unavoidable, considering the definition of the response employed:

> Every *discrete*, voiced sound produced by S was counted as a *vocalization*. A number of other sounds characteristically made by very young infants, e.g. straining sounds and coughs, and the whistles, squeaks and snorts of noisy breathing, were not counted as vocalizations. Sounds falling under the categories of protests, fusses, and cries . . . were recorded separately. No attempt was made to record any of the phonetic characteristics of any of the sounds or their duration (p. 69).

Their definition of the response precludes the use of an electronic voice key, apart from other disadvantages implicit in that device. (A voice key, an electronic switch which is activated by sounds, allows for objective recording and instantaneous reinforcement programming. However, it also records, programs, and reinforces any stray sounds of sufficient intensity to be picked up, like chair squeaks, passing autos, dropped reinforcers, footsteps, or apparatus pounding.)

A second observer checked the reliability of the investigator's judgments, and the investigator and the observer traded roles for half the subjects, as a further check on their mutual reliability. Their percentage of agreement ranged from 67 to 100, with a median of 96, over some 27 three-minute periods involving 13 subjects. The infants were observed lying on their backs in their cribs. The unit of observation was a three-minute period, usually grouped in blocks of three, separated by two-minute rest periods during which the investigators moved away from the crib. An attempt was made to have three such blocks of observation every day: early morning, late morning, and after lunch.

The first two days of study constituted an operant level or baseline period, during which the investigator stood by the baby's crib looking down at him for three-minute periods with "an expressionless face," while the observer (out of the baby's sight) tallied vocalizations.

During the second two days of the study, vocalizations were reinforced by a smile, the sounds of "tsk, tsk, tsk," and a light touch to the baby's abdomen. If the rate of vocalization increased sufficiently, reinforcement was then given after every second response or on a fixed ratio of 2 and after every third response or on a fixed ratio of 3 (but this was rare). The third two days of the study were an extinction period, identical in procedure to the first two days of baseline.

The two days of reinforcement significantly increased the rate to nearly double the baseline rate; two days of extinction returned the rate to very nearly the baseline level. The experiment was duplicated with minor changes, and the results were similar in both sets of observations.

The authors suggest, consequently, that infants' vocal behavior can be brought under experimental control and that a social event composed of ordinary acts performed by a relatively strange adult can function rather quickly as a reinforcer. They carefully point out, however, that concluding that vocalization is an operant requires control observations of a condition in which the reinforcer is given as frequently but not contingent upon the response. Results obtained under this condition, when compared with the results reported, would indicate whether the social stimuli used served to reinforce the infant's preceding response (operant interaction) or to elicit the succeeding one (respondent interaction).

A recent study by Weisberg (1963) contributes such additional information on vocalizing behavior in the infant. Using methods similar to those of Rheingold, Gewirtz, and Ross, but incorporating a period in which random, noncontingent reinforcement was given, Weisberg showed that vocalizing was relatively less affected by such social reinforcers when given freely to infants of this age than when given by the contingent, reinforcing presentation of these stimuli, immediately following the vocalizing response.

Weisberg summarizes his findings as follows:

> Taking the vocalizing rate in the presence of the unresponsive adult as the operant level, it was found that the behavior could be operantly conditioned by social consequences (the adult briefly touched S's chin and simultaneously smiled at and "talked" to him). Extinction operations subsequently reduced the rate but not to baseline performance. Conditions other than social reinforcement (e.g. presenting the reinforcing stimulus non-contingent upon vocalizing and giving an auditory stimulus in the presence of an unresponding adult both independently of and contingent upon vocalizing) did not seem to control infant vocal behavior (p. 388).

These studies used fairly complex combinations of stimuli. Perhaps not all of the stimuli employed were functional as reinforcers. Further experimental study might show that a much more economical stimulus display accomplishes the same change in behavior. It would be valuable to perform a detailed stimulus analysis; but it is also worthwhile to follow the experimenters' line, and to use as reinforcers reasonable copies of stimulation provided by mothers when their infants smile or vocalize, in order to analyze the effects of typical real-life interactions. Both types of studies are important and needed at this stage of the development of child psychology.

We bring this chapter to a close by pointing out that the development of language or verbal behavior has much in common with the development of motor skills. Just as the baby comes to reach, grasp, and retrieve objects, just as he learns to manage the movements of parts of his body, and just as he learns to move about, so he learns to make use of an incredible number of sounds with his vocal equipment. Although the mechanics involved in making the responses are different, gross motor skills and language responses are similar in two important respects: (1) both are closely tied in with biological development (maturation), especially and particularly during the early formative years, and (2) both are sensitive to stimulus consequences; they function as operants.

REFERENCES

Irwin, O. C. Research on speech sounds for the first six months of life. *Psychol. Bull.*, 1941, *38*, 277–285.

McCarthy, Dorothea. Language development in children. In L. Carmichal (Ed.), *Manual of child psychology.* (2nd ed.) New York: Wiley, 1954.

Osgood, C. E. *Method and theory in experimental psychology.* New York: Oxford Univer. Press, 1953.

Rheingold, Harriet L., Gewirtz, J. L., and Ross, Helen W. Social conditioning of vocalizations in the infant. *J. abn. soc. Psychol.*, 1959, 52, 68–73.

Shirley, Mary. *The first two years: III. Personality manifestations.* Minneapolis, Minn.: Univer. of Minn. Press, 1933.

Skinner, B. F. *Verbal behavior.* New York: Appleton-Century-Crofts, 1957.

Weisberg, Paul. Social and nonsocial conditioning of infant vocalizations. *Child Develpm.*, 1963, *34*, 377–388.

11

Early Repertories of Emotional Behavior

In Volume I emotional behavior was described as largely respondent in nature, and closely tied to reinforcement and extinction operations (Vol. I, Ch. 6). In Chapter 3 in this volume, an analysis was made of those repertories of the neonate often called emotional. In this chapter we shall supplement those analyses in two ways: (1) by elaborating on the wider variety of operations which elicit emotional respondents, and (2) by considering in more detail the operant components in emotional interactions.

INTERMINGLING OF OPERANT AND RESPONDENT PROCESSES

Reinforcement Operations

Many reinforcement operations elicit respondent behavior. Presenting positive reinforcers produces "joy," "elation," or "delight"; removing them results in "anger," "grief," or "depression." Presenting negative reinforcers produces "anger" or "fear," and removing them leads to "relief." Whether or not we are satisfied with such labels, those words are commonly attached to the behaviors displayed. The behaviors involved in the interactions are in part respondent, in part operant. The respondent components may consist of blushes, sweating, trembling, changes in breathing rate, goose pimples, and crying. The operant segments commonly include smiles, frowns, verbal statements, gestures, and, quite often, forceful, vigorous, even violent motor behavior. The development of emotional behavior from infancy to adulthood involves the intermingled processes of both operant and respondent conditioning.

In the young infant, the variety of emotional responses is simpler than the foregoing description. A large class of reinforcement operations produces "distress"; another large class produces "delight." The infant in distress cries and thrashes, turns red, arches his back, and markedly changes his breathing rhythm. The delighted baby smiles, makes soft gurgling or cooing sounds, and is in general relaxed. (See discussion of the neonate, Vol. II, Ch. 3.)

However, this description is adequate for only a few months of initial development. Increasingly the baby displays these responses in relation to a wider and wider range of stimulus operations, and increasingly he displays them in more and more fragmented and differentiated forms.

The first kind of elaboration takes place as part of the development we have sketched in the preceding chapters. At first, emotional respondents which are elicited by reinforcement operations are limited to the number and variety of reinforcers effective for the infant (Chapter 6). In a world which contains numerous stimuli as discriminative for those reinforcers, however, a corresponding richness of acquired reinforcers results (Vol. I, pp. 53–58). Acquired reinforcers, like unlearned or homeostatic ones, elicit emotional respondents. As the process of discrimination proceeds, involving physical, chemical, organismic, and social stimuli, emotional behaviors become related to those stimuli to a corresponding degree. Thus emotional behavior is expanded in its range of occurrence not only by respondent conditioning (Chapter 5), but also by the discrimination contingencies which develop acquired reinforcers for operant conditioning.

The second kind of emotional elaboration that takes place involves the increasingly detailed forms which emotional behaviors come to display. Katherine Bridges (1932) gave descriptions of the flowering of the forms of emotional expression. For the first few weeks of life, she said, the emotional displays of an infant might be termed *excitement;* before three months of age, however, a *delighted* and a *distressed* form of excitement appear. In the course of six months of development, distress is differentiated into patterns which might be called *anger, disgust,* and *fear*. After about a year of development, delight might be subdivided into *elation* in some cases, and *affection* in others; and shortly before the second birthday, *joy* becomes a third form of delight. A few months prior to the second birthday *jealousy* appears as a new form of distress.

The elaboration of emotional responses described by Bridges is due in part to the appearance of new behaviors corresponding to the growth and strengthening of the baby's biological equipment. An even greater part, however, is due to the growing complexity of stimuli which elicit respondent behaviors, to the cultural meaning of those stimuli to an observer, and to the increasing role of operant interactions.

As stimuli become discriminative for reinforcement, they acquire reinforcing functions. They may, at one and the same time, have eliciting functions. Suppose a child is playing with his mother and the phone rings. The mother immediately stops playing and goes to answer the phone. If such an event is a consistent characteristic of the child's environment, then the phone bell might be discriminative for the loss of positive reinforcement, playing with his mother. The phone bell would function both to weaken operant behavior and to elicit respondent behavior, perhaps whimpering. The elicited, emotional response component would probably be called *distress*.

Suppose that the situation were altered so that the crying of a baby sibling was the instigator for stopping the mother's play, rather than the ringing of the phone. The same discrimination would take place, and the baby sibling's cry would become both a conditioned negative reinforcer and an eliciting stimulus for the emotional respondent for the child. Under these circumstances, however, the child's reactions would probably be called jealousy rather than distress, because the sibling baby might well be the object of jealousy, not the phone bell. Thus the cultural meaning of relationships with sibling babies and phone bells determines whether a response will be given one label or another. However, as the child grows older, he may learn that a phone bell means some person is calling mother, and we may again label his distress reaction (however he may display it) as jealousy, now that a human agency is again seen by the child as playing the crucial role in his loss of reinforcement.

The increasing role of operant behavior in situations which we classify as emotional may be further developed within the context of chain-breaking, a form of extinction.

Chain-Breaking and Extinction

An operant chain is a sequence of operant responses and stimuli in which each response produces a stimulus which is reinforcing for that response and discriminative for the next one in the chain, until a terminal reinforcement is produced or removed (perhaps not every time, but according to some reinforcement schedule). Dialing a telephone is an example. The dialing of each number is discriminative for the subsequent dialing of the next number, until the chain is completed and either somebody answers or a busy signal occurs. Opening a door is another example: One steps forward, grasps the knob, turns, hears a click or feels the freeness of the door, pushes or pulls until it opens, and then either walks through or stands back to let someone else through.

To break a chain is to terminate it before completion. Thus, chain-breaking is extinction. We have already pointed out that some of the effects of extinction are (1) an eventual reduction in the strength of the previously occurring response and (2) an evocation of respondent behavior, at least in some instances. Let us examine this process further as it relates to the development of emotional repertories.

Chain-breaking may occur in one of two ways. First, the reinforcing stimulus at the end of the chain, which is the one that supports the entire chain, may not occur. Second, a response anywhere in the chain may not produce its usual stimulus consequence; that is, it may fail to produce the discriminative stimulus necessary for the next response in the chain to occur.

The first chain-breaking procedure, non-occurrence of the ultimate reinforcer, would be expected to weaken the whole chain after sufficient repetitions. Chain-breaking of this sort would also be expected to bring about one or several classes of respondent behavior (often called "frustration"). The study by Marquis (1931) referred to in Chapter 3 provides an example of the role of these factors in a study of newborn infants. Marquis observed the behavior of seven infants just before feeding, and at several points during the course of feeding when they were prevented momentarily from sucking. Crying was loud and rapid just prior to feeding, a testimony to the eliciting power of deprivation for emotional behavior. The babies were interrupted by withdrawing the nursing bottle from their mouths after one quarter, one half, and three quarters of it had been ingested. Each successive interruption, a breaking of the sucking chain, produced crying, but less than the preceding interruption had. This was probably due to the diminishing reinforcing effectiveness of the milk as the infant approached satiation (Vol. I, pp. 64–66). Thus chain-breaking was demonstrated to elicit emotional respondents, in degree and kind according to the other aspects of the situation in which it was observed.

The second way chains may be broken also produces the same type of dual consequences, even though the operation disrupts the stimulus-response sequence well in advance of the occurrence of the ultimate reinforcement. A baby may have developed chains which allow him to reach accurately for objects and bring them to him. Many things could happen to disrupt the internal parts of such a chain. The target object might move constantly in quick and irregular ways (as some insects do). The chain would be broken in that the reaching response did not produce its usual stimulus consequence, the tactual stimulation produced by embracing the object with the fingers. The target object might be so slippery that it continually escapes from the baby's fingers (like a wet bar of soap), so that the grasping response of the fingers suddenly loses the tactual feed-back from contact with the object. The object might be fastened down too securely for the baby's strength to move it (like wet candy left too long on a table top). Thus in all three of these cases the chain would be broken, since the arm response of bringing the object to the mouth is mechanically impossible. Each example involves not only nonreinforcement but also the disruption of a chain which has usually led to some reinforcer.

As has been seen, the emotional behavior displayed as a consequence of chain-breaking is often of the distressed type—crying, fretting, or screaming, and abrupt and aimless waving of the arms and kicking of the legs. Occasionally, however, the emotional behavior is of the "pleased" sort—smiling, giggling, and laughing, and vocal crowing. This second kind of emotional response would be likely to occur when a chain is broken and a reinforcer occurs nevertheless. A baby reaching for his first jack-in-the-box might trip the lid bringing the toy to him. This "accident" breaks the chain, in that the child stops, but his reaction to this unexpected event sets up a new chain that may be described as delight rather than dismay.

As chains are developed in greater number and variety, the possible ways of breaking them are similarly increased. Thus, as motor development progresses it will be possible for chains to break completely or only partially, with the corresponding possibility of intense, mild, or no emotional respondent elicitation.

Emotional development is largely conditioned by means of both respondent and operant processes. If there are stimuli consistently antecedent to chain-breaking, then the emotional respondents associated with chain-breaking may be conditioned to these stimuli. Thus certain objects which are characteristically difficult to manipulate with the fingers may become conditioned eliciting stimuli for emotional respondents. They do so because of frequent occurrences of abortive experiences with these objects. A baby may cry on the mere sight of some of his toys.

As the infant has more experience it is likely that more of the behavior he displays in chain-breaking situations is operant in nature. An infant's chain is frequently broken simply because he is not strong enough to manipulate his environment sufficiently to produce some reinforcing outcome. When his chain fails and an emotional display ensues, part of the reaction may involve vigorous flapping motions of the arms and kicking movements of the legs. Sometimes, these vigorous responses overcome the obstacle and so produce reinforcement. The operant components of the emotional behavior displayed will be strengthened by such occurrences. Thus such events may act to shape vigorous responses in general, and strong behavior in particular on occasions of chain-breaking. The breaking of the chain under the latter circumstances serves as the discriminative stimulus for more vigorous behavior. To the extent that the physical world can be modified to produce reinforcement simply by exerting more effort, the pattern of response to chain-breaking will be strong and will generalize to other chains. There is a suggestion here as to how some forms of so-called aggressive behavior develop.

Emotional Behaviors Accompanying Homeostatic Reinforcement

Most chains end in reinforcement. Displays of delight or joy elicited by reinforcers at the end of chains are not uncommon. Frequently (and especially in the early months of child development) emotional responses of delight are seen *during* the course of ongoing chains. Emotional responses of this sort are likely to occur on occasions of the first successful mastery of previously difficult chains, because of the previous history of respondent conditioning. As the chain is strengthened the stimuli involved in it not only become firmly discriminative for the next responses in the chain, but they may also acquire both reinforcing and eliciting functions on the basis of their temporal relationships to the ultimate reinforcing stimulus.

In addition to reinforcing the entire chain, many terminal stimuli elicit an emotional respondent; hence many stimuli in the chain may bear the proper temporal relationship to the terminal stimuli to permit respondent conditioning. The stimuli occurring previously in the chain become conditioned eliciting stimuli, and the emotional respondents they elicit occur earlier in the chain. Through higher-order conditioning (and this is highly speculative, as pointed out in Chapter 5), respondent behavior can move forward in time, with decreasing strength, to any point in the chain.

Thus the elaboration of operant behavior into longer and longer chains of well-coordinated responses is accompanied by a corresponding elaboration of emotional behavior, both in the range of stimulus situations in which emotional responses occur and in the gradations and intensities displayed.

Chain-Breaking and Negative Reinforcement

Suppose a chain is not merely broken but in addition a negative reinforcer is presented at the same moment. For example, a toddler has been deriving a great deal of satisfaction from dragging a pull toy about the room on a string. In addition to its movement, the toy changes color and makes melodic sounds as it rolls along. On one occasion the toy becomes entangled in the legs of the couch and stops. The youngster yanks hard on the string, which breaks, and he falls on the floor and bumps his head. The usual toy-playing chain has broken and a negative reinforcer has been imposed simultaneously. The processes described in the preceding paragraphs would be expected to operate, but with more intensity. The negative reinforcer itself would elicit emotional respondents, as would the chain-breaking; in combination, an intense display of emotional behavior would be expected. Operant behavior which avoids chain-breaking or repairs a chain is likely to be modified by such incidents, as is operant behavior which avoids negative reinforcers like a blow to the head. Operant conditioning is expected to develop rapidly under such circumstances and to be more enduring.

DEPRIVATION, SATIATION, AND OTHER SETTING EVENTS FOR EMOTIONAL BEHAVIOR

A stimulus may elicit emotional respondents on one occasion but not on another. All the reasons for such variability are hardly understood at present, but at least some can be analyzed. One of the most common factors that play a part is the infant's state of deprivation or satiation for homeostatic reinforcers like food or water.

The deprived child, in this respect, is likely to display emotional behaviors to a wide variety of stimuli. Some of these stimuli would not elicit emotional displays on other occasions. For example, tickling a child may ordinarily produce laughter and other manifestations of delight, but tickling a hungry child as a distraction technique may produce a storm of crying, and, in some instances, a full-blown tantrum. Some of these behaviors are respondent, and are more readily elicited under conditions of deprivation. Some are operant. The contingencies under which they may develop are as follows: when a child is hungry, a tantrum may move the parent to feed the child promptly, especially if the parent is convinced that the child's irritability is a simple consequence of his hunger. In effect, the tantrum behavior follows the formula of a discriminated operant. In the presence of an organismic discriminative stimulus (deprivation), a class of operants (tantrum) produces a positive reinforcer (food).

Other stimuli which usually elicit emotional respondents will do so even with greater strength under conditions of deprivation. Conversely, under conditions of satiation, they would do so minimally. The recently fed child typically is more tolerant of chain-breaking and negative reinforcers than under other conditions; if hurt, his cries are briefer, and his distractibility greater.

Sleep cycles show a similar function. The infant who has been awake a long time is easily stimulated to cry, fret, and otherwise display emotion; the sleep-satisfied child is more difficult to provoke. Even after a child's sleep cycle has stabilized into the usual adult pattern, conditions of rest and fatigue will play an analogous role.

Heat and cold show similar effects on the elicitation of emotional respondents. Indeed, any period of prolonged stimulation involving negative reinforcers, or fairly intense stimulation in any sense modality (e.g., lights, sounds, pressures), may constitute a setting event for emotional displays. It is common to hear parents remark that a fretful child has been "overstimulated."

In all these examples, it is important to keep in mind what the *consequences* of an emotional display may be. To the extent that the emotional responses are respondent, this consideration will not be important, since respondents are not sensitive to stimulus consequences. However, operants and respondents do not occur in isolation. For one thing, respondents often are elicited by reinforcement operations, and the presence of reinforcers usually is discriminative for operants which secure or avoid them. For another thing, operant behavior goes on almost constantly. Consequently, any emotional situation is likely to be one in which operant behavior too is being developed. This is perhaps nowhere so true as in social situations.

Many of the emotional displays of infants are highly reinforcing to adults. The delight of a child may inspire the development of complex skills in a parent, simply to produce that delight in the youngster more often; and at the same time, parents may learn a large repertory of responses which terminate or avoid the baby's aversive crying, whimpering, and fretting behavior. Thus, emotional behavior typically is followed by a multitude of actions by adults, many involving reinforcement operations. Operant responses involved in the baby's emotional displays will be affected by these reinforcement contingencies. A common consequence is the development of whimpering and tantrums as a reinforced behavior, one which both escapes from negative reinforcers and also secures positive reinforcers which the parents would not otherwise give.

REFERENCES

Bridges, K. M. B. Emotional development in early childhood. *Child Develpm.*, 1932, *3*, 324–341.

Marquis, Dorothy P. Can conditioned responses be established in the newborn infant? *J. genet. Psychol.*, 1931, *39*, 479–492.

12

Summary — and a Look Forward

A systematic and empirical theory of behavioral development, presented in Volume I of *Child Development*, has been applied in Volume II to an analysis of the first stage of human development. This phase, labeled the Universal stage, begins in the fetal period with the onset of unified activity and ends at the time symbolic behavior becomes prominent. It is characterized by (1) the initial prevalence of biological activity and functioning, (2) the establishment of simple respondent and operant behaviors, and (3) the beginnings of ecological behavior, or first-order adjustment behavior. The manifestation of ecological behavior is dependent on prior and concurrent respondent and operant development; it is in fact an elaboration of them.

Analysis of prenatal development suggests that the psychological history of the individual begins during the latter part of the fetal period. The extent and significance of changes in psychological behavior before birth are very much questions rather than facts, and definite conclusions must be postponed until further reliable experimental data are available.

A survey of the stimulus-response relationships during the first postnatal week reveals that the infant is reactive to light, sound, odor, temperature, electric shock, pin pricks, solutions applied to the tongue, and bodily orientation and movement. It is not yet clear whether during this period these reactions can be conditioned in a stable manner either by respondent or operant procedures. It has been demonstrated, however, that the strength of these initial interactions is modifiable. Continual presentation of many of the eliciting stimuli brings about adaptation (decrements in responding). Furthermore, certain precurrent and simultaneous setting events such as aversive stimulation, and deprivation of and satiation for food and water, sleep, and air bring about changes in the latency amplitude.

It is also apparent that sudden and strong stimulation, or disruptions in behavior chains closely related to biological functioning, produce external and internal changes that might collectively be labeled "excitement." On the other hand, low-level prolonged stimulation, and satiation for primary reinforcers, result in external and internal changes that might be called "quiescence."

Respondent and operant processes are manifested shortly after the neonatal period, albeit in a fairly unstable manner. On the rather safe assumption that the preponderance of the behavior changes included in pyschological development is of the operant kind, an analysis of such behaviors requires knowledge of the kinds of reinforcers that are effective in shaping gross motor, social, and verbal responses and in bringing them under the initial discriminating and reinforcing control. For the most part, the environmental events involved in these interactions are closely associated with care-taking activities of the mother and the biological functioning of the infant. On the further assumption that what is generally referred to as emotional development is for the most part a combination of respondent and operant processes, an analysis requires delineation of those stimulating conditions, reactions, and setting events that apparently are involved in the early displays of emotion.

Although each infant is unique in his total anatomical structure and physiological functioning, there is considerable similarity in the behavioral changes that take place during the Universal stage. Throughout most of this period, the infant is functioning primarily as a biological organism, and much of the behavior displayed is common to his species characteristics. His contacts with the social and physical events are for the most part related to optimizing his biological functioning. For all infants, too, the social and physical environments are fairly homogeneous, not only because of the similarity in limitations imposed by extreme biological immaturity but also because of the extensive uniformity in infant-caring practices.

The next objective is to apply the principles described in Volume I to an analysis of behavior during the next three or four years of development. This period is called the Basic stage. During the Basic stage, the biological structure of a child is more effective for interacting with the environment, and his biological functioning is more efficient and less compelling. Therefore, more opportunity is provided and greater energy is available for the development of psychological behaviors. What repertories will be developed in a youngster will depend greatly on the social conditions which prevail in his family, the major source of relevant stimulating variables. Other sources are, of course, the child's biological make-up, in which hereditary processes play a significant role, and the influences from other people in the home and in the immediate community.

It is during the Basic stage that many of the individually unique ways of behaving are established, i.e., the "personality structure" is fabricated. Almost all the activities of the mother (not just those involved in care-taking) and other members of the family may provide occasions and contingencies which guide the young child in acquiring his basic discriminations and forms of behavior. The family is often said to be the child's first educational institution, which, through informal and formal procedures, teaches him selected discriminations; selected motor and verbal skills and repertories beyond simple prehension, locomotion, manding and tacting behaviors; social-role response systems, food likes and dislikes, activity preferences, interests, and "temperamental" characteristics; and emotional repertories, especially in relation to conditioned aversive stimulation and positive reinforcement following deprivation. While specific interactions are being acquired, the individual's general style of behaving is also being developed. These and related topics will be the subject matter of Volume III.

INDEX